The
BIBLE
of
LOVE

How to Stop F*cking Yourself Over & Start Making Love - To Yourself, To Her, and To Life

MARINA LAZARIS

The Bible of Love: How to Stop F*cking Yourself Over and Start Making Love—
to Yourself, to *Her*, and to *Life*

ISBN: 979-8-89694-397-6 - ebook
ISBN: 979-8-89694-398-3 - paperback
ISBN: 979-8-89694-506-2 - hardcover

FROM FEAR TO LOVE

♡

I'm sorry,

Please forgive me,

Thank you,

I love you.

This is Ho'oponopono, an ancient Hawaiian prayer for forgiveness. 'Ho'oponopono' roughly translates to "move things back in balance" and "make things right".

Powerfully simplistic. It brought tears to my eyes when I shared it with my loved ones. I encourage you to experience how repeating it as part of a daily practice shifts your subconscious and heals your relationship with yourself and others.

Your prayer will be beautifully unique to you, my dear reader. Mine goes something like this:

~

I'm sorry for not nurturing the masculine within me, being unable to show up fully for the men in my life because I couldn't show up for myself.

Please forgive me for criticising myself for not 'doing' or 'being' enough, causing myself pain instead of peace.

Thank you to all of the incredible men who have protected, provided and cared for me unconditionally. Thank you for what I have learnt, and for the honour of letting me share my experiences with you.

I love you with all of my heart. I hope you heal and rise once more back to your soul.

I love you.

Contents

THE WAY YOU MAKE LOVE IS THE WAY YOU LIVE YOUR LIFE.

(13) What is the difference between fucking and making love?

(14) I've slept with plenty of women and never had any complaints, so I can't be doing that badly?!

(15) Why can't I seem to separate pain and pleasure anymore?

FANTASIES

(16) Should I feel guilty for having a fantasy?

(17) Cool, but what about sexual fantasies?

(18) I'm on a hamster wheel of porn and empty sex. Is there a way out?

(19) How do I create connection and break the cycle?

(SIXTY)NINE TO FIVE

(21) What's the secret recipe for being in a successful relationship?

(22) How do I keep things exciting?

(23) Why don't my relationships ever last longer than one year?

(24) Is my childhood affecting my adult relationships?

(25) Should I stay or should I go?

(26) I can't forgive my ex for the pain they caused me and the time they wasted.

(27) Why can't I seem to 'get over it' or move on?

(28) *How* do I move on?

(29) I'm terrified of getting hurt again!

DIVORCE

INTRODUCTION

Cast your mind back to your best friend's 6th birthday party, the "When I Grow Up" themed one. I'm pretty sure none of us ate cake and played Musical Statues dressed as a victim. Sure, you might've been a pilot, a footballer, or even a lion. But you certainly weren't aspiring to live a life of victimhood. So, why do we continue choosing this as adults? I'd much rather be a lion.

Since having my second child, I've woken up. I realised I'd been fucking myself over. I learned that, eventually, getting the change you want and *need* requires leaving the victimhood behind. Instead, you need to grab your life by the balls, step up and take responsibility. That's when things shift from general fuckery to sweet, sweet love-making.

I appreciate that me telling you to ditch the victimhood so soon is bold. But that's reality, right? And it forms the basis of The Subconscious Rise Method: my unique coaching method that leads you back to a fulfilled life by showing you how I learned to Love the Fuck out of Everything (more on that later).

While being a relationship coach that was born on Valentine's Day makes for *great* marketing fodder, I'm not about to start preaching like I've got some kind of crystal ball with all the answers. The world of love, sex and relationships is complicated. You won't catch me telling you it isn't. Instead, I'll give you a different, straight-talking perspective. I will confront you, challenge you to think differently, and offer an alternative to the damaging narratives that are consuming our society and demonising masculinity. Because, guess what: men need love too, now more than ever. And with the rate of male suicide continuing to be swept under the rug, it's about time someone said it.

I advise approaching each chapter with an open mind and a readiness to break out of the boxes you're trapped in. Absorb it, then make your own mind up.

Maybe life doesn't need to be a series of "either/or". How about "yes, and…". How about a life where you stop judging yourself and others, put two fingers up to society's version of happiness and perfection, and start daring? Daring to trust your gut, to love yourself, to fuck up? Wouldn't *that* be a life lived fully…

1

FOR THE LOVE OF SELF

---

(1) Who do you think you are?

Imagine yourself centre stage, under a massive fucking spotlight. Now, with all your past, passions, dreams, desires, thoughts and little quirks exposed: Who are you?

You might be thinking –

> *"I have no idea how to answer that."* Or perhaps;
> *"I feel like I'm different things to different people, but I have no clue who I am to me…"*

Welcome aboard. There is no shame in feeling confusion around this and you're certainly not the only one. Most of us spend our lives bumbling along with no foundational knowledge of who in the hell we actually are. Go team.

Perhaps you're "The Boss" at work, "Dad" at home, "The Lover" in the bedroom, then "Jack the Lad" at the pub. And you wouldn't be wholly to blame. Society's requirement for us to play different characters at different moments in our lives is deeply ingrained. Most of us play them so convincingly, we deserve an Oscar. That's all well and good, but it's often so subconscious that our answer to "Who are You?" consists of… awkward silence, at best.

In wafting through life, seamlessly transitioning from one role to the next, we forget to cast ourselves in the main role of…drumroll please… *Human.* The part where we fuck up, we learn, we grow. The part where we stop squashing ourselves into each environment's box, but instead show up with integrity as our whole selves, wherever we are. Fuck the boxes. Be all of it – Boss, Dad, the Lover *and* the Lad – all at the same time. Drop the act and just be *you*.

The other trap many of us fall into with 'Who am I?' is answering with our job title. "Oh, I'm a… entrepreneur/lawyer/athlete"…you get the gist. On this, I want to share with you the biggest gift my Dad ever gave me:

He taught me that you are not the job you do. You are so much more. Tying your identity to your job is dangerous. You can lose your job in a second and that can call your whole existence into question (he learned this the hard way). You are a human being – a soul living a human experience.

It's about who you are *being*. That's what matters.

Are you being kind? Are you being compassionate? Are you acting in different roles, or are you being *you*? Are you being loving? *That's* the identity no one can take from you. It's who you *were* that leaves a mark in this world. In the end, no one really gives a shit what you *did*.

(2) How do I stop holding myself back and fucking myself over?

You may feel like, in many areas of life, you are not reaching your full potential and you have a lot more to give. The only way you can stop holding yourself back is to stop hating and dismissing parts of yourself. Learn to love the fuck out of yourself. Love a*ll of it*; your passions and pet peeves, your decisions and dark moments, your anxieties and appearance, your past…the whole box and dice. Until you stop rejecting parts of yourself and comparing to what others are doing or achieving, you will continue fucking yourself over.

———

4

Let me offer a simple example. A crippling anxiety to perform in the bedroom can consume someone so completely that it physically manifests into erectile dysfunction. They stop having amazing sexual experiences and lose touch with the excitement that once lit them up. Instead of spiraling, hating their anxiety for robbing them of the opportunity to the fullest possible life, what if they chose to love and thank this anxiety for keeping them safe? Perhaps it's their body's way of saying it no longer wants to 'perform', but wants to be loved just the way it is? Perhaps it's their body's way of stopping them in their tracks before their lifestyle makes them ill? The body should be thanked for that.

You'll be surprised how much both the initial anxiety, and the physical manifestation, begins to fade away once you reframe something you hate about yourself as something you love the fuck out of.

Furthermore, once you view this former obstacle as not only a gift but a *strength,* you will find that you're no longer affected or held back by the opinions of women who tell you they care about that shit, because you're so comfortable, secure and confident in your own skin. To the right women, that's the *sexiest* thing.

Really focus on reframing things you don't like about yourself as one of your superpowers.

Changing your perspective like this makes you so attractive. It's the most powerful, freeing thing you could ever do for yourself.

But no one's going to do it for you.

So, I challenge you: try flipping the script in your own head.

2

FOR THE LOVE OF MANKIND

Ever heard of the old adage, 'The man, the myth, the legend'? Like all the best triplets ('*breakfast, lunch and dinner*' has got to be up there..!), it deserves to be digested bit by bit. In this chapter, we're going to do just that. We'll deep dive into the importance of leaving society's lost, internally-conflicted 'Alpha male' in the rear-view mirror, in favour of reconnecting to the man you are right now, your core values and the answers that lie *within*. Then we'll turn our attention to busting some popular myths. I will offer an alternative perspective that hopefully helps you to cultivate some balance and momentum in your life, no longer held back by fear or confusion. And what about the legendary man you aspire to be? The man your younger self dreamed of being? The man the world needs? Who is this man? This 'Legend'? We're going to bring him to life.

THE MAN

"Boys become men, when they learn to love."

This section is titled 'The Man', not 'The *Men*', very much on purpose. We won't get the desired 'aha moment' out of this book if we pussyfoot around addressing the combative (and, let's be honest, unhelpful as fuck) herd mentality that society is dressing up as "masculinity" at the moment.

The gym-going, business-owning, designer watch-wearing "Alpha male" is being dressed up as the ultimate picture of '*proper* manliness', but it's the blind leading the blind. This narrative is coming from a place of trauma. Men without a strong sense of self are seeking belonging and connection in the wrong places, allowing themselves to be led by the crowd rather than their own values. You're better than that.

You owe it to yourself to keep your eyes wide open. You're no *damsel in distress* needing answers from some knight in shining armour. All the strength, courage and ability needed to heal and choose your path is already within you. Be your own goddamn knight and use it. Regardless of your past, whatever bad things you've done or challenges you've overcome, wear those experiences like a coat of armour. Know that, in each moment, you did the best you could with the tools and knowledge you had. Now I'm giving you new tools, new knowledge, and a new narrative:

You are the hero of your story – don't give that power away.

(3) Great pep talk, Marina. But what if swallowing my opinions and emotions is all I know?

Perhaps you do so completely unconsciously. Maybe you fear that if you give in to your emotions, you won't be able to control yourself? Or perhaps you fear that saying or doing the *wrong* thing could devastate your career, your family, or even your reputation…fair enough. But hear me out:-

The goal in life is not to be happy, but to live fully.

That means, to live the most fulfilled life, you need to:

1. Open up your emotional range to feel *everything*; from joy and lust, to anger and despair.
2. Know how to *release* those emotions.
3. Move past them.

Feel

Showing emotion, having an opinion and even voicing it (heaven forbid) is sexy! Grounded, attractive masculinity combines these things. Embrace emotion, be proud of your opinions and stand by the man you are on the inside. Do all of this with a healthy dose of kindness, too. Stopping yourself from doing so will only create inner turmoil and anguish. No one needs that.

(4) "What if I start crying and can't stop?"

Think of it this way. As quickly as your last belly laugh came and went, your emotions can pass equally as quickly. Just because you cry doesn't mean you're broken. You simply need to let that hormone pass through. The numbness felt by repressing emotion is a huge contributing factor to depression. When you continue squashing your emotions into a box, not letting them pass through, that box will eventually burst. So rather than repressing, let the tears come and let them pass. The same for anger or frustration. It all needs to be felt before it can be released.

Release

(5) "I'm constantly beating myself up, but releasing my emotions sounds like a shit idea. How do I do that without regretting it?"

Step 2 is crucial. Releasing emotions isn't just about talking things through or re-telling the same story over and over. That's coffee-shop talk. Doing that keeps you stuck in your victimhood and strengthens the neuro-pathway, amplifying the emotions and causing you to re-ignite them, rather than releasing them. Not what we're after. Give life to the *feelings* present in your body right now, rather than repeating the past story behind those feelings.

One of my favourite ways to do this is through physical exertion like boxing. However, boxing in silence won't work. The game-changer is connecting the action to the emotion, with each punch. As you punch; who are you imagining hurting? What do you want to say to that person? What needs to be heard? What needs to come out? I invite you to get all of your emotions out. No one ever gives us license to punch *harder*. Scream *louder*.

Here's your license.

Turning to 'hustle and grind' or punishing yourself in the gym is sometimes a trauma response. It's separation, not healing. It comes from not knowing how to work through your emotions, so you start hurting people, mainly yourself. So, rather than *metaphorically* beating yourself and everyone else up, let that shit out for *real* (in a healthy way please, *Sir*). Getting that energy out of your body makes you less of a loaded gun, triggered by everyone and everything (you know, the road-rage type that pops a blood vessel when someone overtakes him wrong). Instead, you'll be more of the man your younger self would've loved.

Move the fuck On

(6) I can't just forgive those that hurt me. Moving on ain't that easy!

I'm going to come in harsh here. At some point, you need to move the fuck on by taking responsibility for the turmoil and chaos you've created in your life. Forgive yourself for not knowing better. Have compassion for the part of you that wanted to control everything and get it right all the time. Congratulate yourself for growing and learning from that experience. It made you the man you are today. It's part of your armour now.

If you want to see change, there needs to be a step to alter your thinking and behaviour, in order to break the cycle so it no longer controls you. You already have the courage within you to take that step, use it. Dig deep and trust that you're resourceful and strong enough to move past it. You have a 100% success rate for surviving every time you've been wronged in the past, why would this be any different?

The importance of moving past negative emotion and reconnecting to the positive isn't as 'airy-fairy' as it sounds. Armour (1991) found that the heart contains around 40,000 sensory neurites, meaning it has a sophisticated nervous system of its own, resembling a "little brain". This little brain has a rhythmic pattern that directly reflects our emotions.[1] Getting stuck in emotions such as stress, fear, anger and frustration causes an incoherent rhythmic pattern that impairs creativity, causes trouble sleeping and disturbs the immune system. Conversely, positive emotions like love, joy and gratitude cause a coherent pattern that enables us to create, learn and make optimal decisions. They also cause deeper intuitive guidance – giving the voice that connects us to our inner wis-

---

1   Waters, J.A, et al, *Single-port laparoscopic right hemicolectomy: the first 100 resection*. Dis Colon Rectum, 2012. 55(2): p. 134-9.

dom a big fat megaphone and re-focusing our lives.[2] Perhaps it's not such a far reach to see that releasing the negative and reconnecting with the positive would be the ultimate 'cheat-code' to living the most purpose-driven, fulfilled life?

(7) But being happy 24/7 just isn't realistic?

Absolutely right. If you believe that everyone's super fucking happy all the time, you're setting yourself up for a very miserable let-down. That carefree, high-on-life exterior is neither real nor sustainable. However, a shit day doesn't have to feel traumatic or chaotic. There is beauty in days like that because the down moments ground us. They help us find wisdom, clarity and certainty – honour that. They remind us that we can't smile and please people all the time, because we're human. Be authentic to how you feel in those low moments, then use the newfound clarity and wisdom to inform how you choose to move forward.

(8) What's something practical to jumpstart me into moving on?

Acting is not given enough credit for the transformative tool it can be in helping to move through emotions and, ultimately, move on. Part of The Subconscious Rise Method uses the closest thing I can offer to a shortcut for moving on. It goes like this:

Team up with a trusted friend that's willing to help you in this process. Act out the situations that hurt you or made you feel powerless, releasing your emotions while you do. If you feel angry, let that anger out. Your friend's only job is to witness this and hold the space for you, with no judgement. Then, re-enact those moments, giving them an alternative ending whereby you regain your power. Then go further. Act out the

---

2   R.McCraty, M.Atkinson, and R.T. Bradley, *Electrophysiological evidence of intuition: Part 2. A system-wide process?* Journal of Alternative and Complementary Medicine, 2004. 10(2): p. 325-336.

character of the person that wronged or mistreated you, stepping into their shoes. By doing this, we explore what it might have been like to be them, make their decisions and do what they did. Often, doing this prompts compassion and the beginning of forgiveness for the person that wronged us. But, more importantly, we start to feel that same forgiveness and compassion for ourselves.

I'll offer a personal example of how powerful and enlightening acting can be as a tool for processing, learning and growing. For me, sex would often get to a point where my partner would have his hands around my throat. I never thought of this as abusive, because I'd never done it to anyone else. However, in a recent acting job, my character was the aggressor. I had to put my hands around someone's neck, for the first time. Whilst 'only acting', it stopped me in my tracks and made me think about what it must be like to do that to someone 'in real life', especially during acts of deep intimacy. I paused. I took this moment in. I questioned why I needed this to 'feel something' and why I'd allowed that to be done to me. I knew, from then on, I wanted intimacy to be a gentler, more beautiful, more magical experience for me. I knew I no longer needed the abusiveness to 'feel'.

I felt compassion for the version of me that allowed it in the past, and forgave myself. Thanks to having acted out the aggressor's role, I developed an understanding of what I'd been creating for myself, and now had total clarity on how I wanted to move forward.

(9) I don't feel comfortable acting stuff out yet. What else is there?

My totally honest response to this question? Get comfortable with it. Moving on in your mind won't truly work until you've processed through your body first – whether that's through boxing, acting or a combination. Only after you've done that can you attempt to move on mentally.

———

When it comes to mental processing, the subconscious is powerful. Your brain goes into Theta State (the essential stage for programming) 10 minutes before sleeping and 10 minutes after waking up. How energy and information is directed through your neural circuits can alter the brain's activity and its' structure."[3] In other words, the things you choose to think, hope, feel and imagine during these 10-minute windows will shape your reality – for better or worse.[4]

Focusing on what you *don't* want will not only attract it, but will create the incoherent rhythmic pattern in your heart that prompts the negative physical responses we've already explored, such as trouble sleeping and weakened immunity. Avoid this by using the 10 minute windows to frame thoughts about what you want in the future as if they are happening *right now*, in the present.

> "Now, I am happy. Now, I am at peace. Now, I love myself. Now, I have everything I need to be fulfilled."

That will change everything. If you're not sure where to start, I'd recommend listening to *'Self Hypnosis to Fucking Freedom & Love'* on Spotify.[5]

---

3 *You Are Not Your Brain: The 4-Step Solution for Changing Bad Habits, Ending Unhealthy Thinking, and Taking Control of Your Life;* Jeffrey M. Schwartz (2012).

4 *Scients Proves Your Thoughts Influence Your Reality and Shape Your Brain for Better or Worse. You Choose.;* Debbie Hampton (2022), https://thebestbrainpossible.com/thoughts-brain-neuroplasticity-reality/

5 *Self Hypnosis to Fucking Freedom & Love;* The Marina Show, Marina Lazaris (2023).

THE MYTHS

There's a *lot* of misconceptions plaguing our subconscious, and our society. And we aren't at fault for that. For the large majority, so much of our lives, time, money and energy is now spent online. This means that, by default, we absorb a lot more misguided information that we realise. Then, thanks to simply being human, we internalise many of the myths so deeply, our brains accept them as truths before we know it. I'm not here to judge or get on a soapbox and call these storylines wrong. In fact, quite the opposite. There's something to be said about the sense of vision and purpose they bring when it comes to *going somewhere* in life.

Perhaps the problem isn't the myths themselves, but the lack of alternative viewpoints out there balancing and challenging them, offering you the luxury of considering different options and making your own mind up? After all, imagine paying top dollar for a swanky continental breakfast, only to be offered a choice of fried egg or, err, fried egg. It'd be bloody boring.

So, with the aim of bringing some balance to the table, let's dig in. Relationship coach by day, Myth Buster by night…

Myth #1: Having the car, the women, the house and the "next best thing" will make me powerful, successful and happy.

You may think that nailing the gym, making good money, having status and "dress[ing] like a Mafia Boss"[6] makes you the fucking Catch of the Day, and you'd be spot on. It'll make you exactly that, catch of the *day*. I'm going to take a gamble and assume it's not just me who'd rather be the Catch of a *Lifetime*. As I said, chasing this myth isn't all bad. You might be lucky enough to land up with a shiny new suit that's

---

6   A. Tate (2022)

---

a little tight around the biceps and a car that wakes the neighbours. But, you will attract women wanting a slice of these superficial things, rather than those wanting to know and love the man you are inside. Your interactions with them will start resembling a trade-off, a back and forth exchange of power and sex. This 'works well' for some in the short term. However, the transactional backdrop will lead to a loss of respect on both sides. Most importantly, you'll lose respect for yourself as you burn through these women quickly and slip further away from finding the raw, genuine love you deserve.

Sound familiar? You wouldn't be the first whose chase after external success has been rudely interrupted by a feeling of emptiness he can't shake.

My dad, my hero, once said to me, "Marina! Life begins at 40!" The little girl in me thought – "Great! Soon, his life will start. Soon, he's going to be happy. Soon, Mum and Dad will love each other again!" I even made posters and threw him a party. His 40th birthday came. His life never…began. Instead, not only did he feel the same void he did at 39, but he was diagnosed with a pituitary gland tumour and nearly died. He felt like he was totally missing out on the *magic sauce* others seemed to have in life. He had all the pieces society told him he needed; the successful business, the wife, the 2.2 kids. But they weren't piecing together the "happy" picture he was promised. In all honesty, he was working 7 days a week and felt pretty pissed off with the world. He'd been sold a lie that left him completely disconnected inside.

Blinded by pushing for external security, Dad could no longer see pain inside himself. He never stopped to breathe. In striving to become the man society told him to be, he neglected himself and his needs entirely. He lost sight of looking after the man that needed nurturing the most, the man inside. Learn Dad's lesson. Prioritise what You want…not what the herd wants. Prioritise the Man…not the Men.

(10) That's all very well, but what else am I meant to chase?

The most valuable thing you can do is *reconnect* to the man you are inside, at your very core. Women aside, what are your turn-ons and passions? What makes you tick? If you struggle to answer these, try this one on for size: What do you want to leave behind in the world?

These are the things that no one can trade or take from you. Take a moment to brainstorm and establish what these things are, then stop thinking and start *doing*. Pick up the instrument you used to love playing as a kid. Start volunteering for your local food bank. Offer to coach or referee a few games for the local kids football club. Doing these things will lift you out of the transactional cycle of being a man with *tradeable* qualities. Instead, by breathing life into the things that make you *you,* you become a man that is so confident and proud of what you're creating in the world, you abandon all 'trade-offs' in favour of only engaging with women who have passions, ambitions and legacies of their own. These women will be turned on by the person you are, enter into a relationship because of what can be built together, and be far less interested in what they can *trade* with you. Enter, stage left, the *equal* exchange of power and respect that characterises real love and peaceful relationships that go the distance.

Myth #2: The 'Perfect Woman' exists. She's just hiding somewhere...

No, sunshine. You are setting yourself up for a disappointing innings if you believe there's a 'perfect' woman anywhere. There isn't. And guess what, there's no 'perfect' man out there either. We're human. Seeking and expecting perfection from others (and yourself, for that matter) is going to land you in a shallow, brown puddle of BORING. You're here for more than boring. You *deserve* more than boring. It's imperfections that make each of us precious, interesting and lovable. So yeah, fuck perfection.

Now that's out the way... I want to address *The List*. You know, the tick-box exercise of all the qualities your 'ideal woman' has. Let me guess:

- ☑ Easy on the eye
- ☑ Brain cells (plural)
- ☑ Wizard in the kitchen
- ☑ Funny (but not *too* funny)
- ☑ Same cultural wavelength
- ☑ Lady in the streets, freak in the sheets?

Reading that, you've probably built up a nice, vivid picture of her in your head. Now I want you to inhale...exhale...and TEAR UP the god-damn list! Not because you can't find a woman with some (or all!) of those qualities. Sure, maybe you can – go you. But, listen. You can far quicker waste years of your life falling in love with the *version* of her you created on your list, not who she *really* is. Inevitably, she'll go about living her life based on the reality of who she is (how dare she), while you grow increasingly frustrated and resentful that she's not meeting your expectations or following the script *you* conjured up in your head. Then what? Being the playwright that you are, you start trying to mould her like a ball of clay and get her to *'stick to the script, for fuck's sake'*! If you're lucky and there's genuine love there, she'll push back. Why? Because love is not control, possession or expectations. None of the shit in your list will matter when you're old and grey. Do yourself a favour. Let it go.

(11) If my list is bollocks, how am I meant to recognise Mrs Right?

When it comes to recognising someone you *should* invest your time into, my best advice is to focus on the person your gut is gravitating towards. The person your soul connects to. The person you could enjoy a silent cuppa with. *That* connection is paramount.

And when you think you might've found her? *Lean in* to your masculine energy with reckless abandon. Pick up the phone and *pursue her*. Consistently. *Fearlessly.* Do so in the knowledge that you are worthy and deserving of love. Do so in the knowledge that, even if she doesn't return the same feelings, your life will still be better for having a meaningful, authentic *friendship* with her. Take it from a woman; if you've torn up the list, paid attention to *connection* and picked up the phone, you're already miles ahead of the competition and will stand out as a far superior man...go on, legend.

THE LEGEND

Finally, The Legend. The climax of this chapter. The Legend is the pinnacle of mankind, the ultimate man of substance, the man soaked in expensive champagne on the top of life's podium.

Spoiler – it's not the guy everyone thinks.

This is a man who isn't scared of emotional connection or vulnerability. In fact, he embraces it with open arms, understanding that connection with his own and others' emotions unlocks the ability to live the fullest, most satisfying life in every aspect; his work, his play, his pleasure. This is a man deeply connected to who he is, who takes action on his passions, desires and core beliefs. He thinks for himself and is led by his intuition, uninfluenced by what society tells him he should be desiring or believing. This is a man who knows inner peace and embodies total authenticity. He is powerful, and attractive as fuck.

In healing every false thought or small idea he's had about himself, he replaced a fear of being rejected with a quiet confidence that rejection has nothing to do with him and everything to do with what the other person is working through. He stopped running away from deeper, more vulnerable connections, and started listening closely when his heart told him to run *towards* the passions, purpose and people that light him up.

I'm not just waxing lyrical for the sake of it. Imagining something activates the same neurons and brain chemicals as experiencing it for real.[7] Neuroscientific research by Mangers & Altenmüller (2003) validated that visualisation practice influences physical changes from muscle

---

7   *Modulation of muscle responses evoked by transcranial magnetic stimulation during the acquisition of new fine motor skills;* A Pascual-Leone, D Nguyet, L G Cohen, J P Brasil-Neto, A Commarota, M Hallet (1995).

strength to brain pathways.[8] So, if you're able to imagine yourself on a beach, humour me and follow the journey I'm about to take you on. You'll find you already know a legend like this, pretty well in fact.

Close your eyes. Place your hands firmly on your heart.

Imagine a green colour radiating from your heart. It forms a protective, energy shield around you.

Take a deep breath, releasing any tension as you exhale. Allow yourself to fully relax.

From this moment forward, you are fully forgiven for ignoring your body, its gifts and its wisdom in the past. Your body wants you to listen now, and know that you are truly loved.

Notice where you still have tension in your body. The green light is now a beam, radiating out of your heart, melting that tension away.

Let every piece of your body feel relaxed.

Another deep breath now, letting go.

Keeping your hands on your heart and eyes closed, imagine you are transported to a beautiful beach. Sink your feet into the sand. Feel the sun on your face as it warms your entire body.

Hear the sound of the waves gently rolling onto the shore. You can almost taste the sea air and feel completely at peace.

Your heart is now in flow and you are ready to meet your Inner Legend.

---

8   *Mapping perception to action in piano practice: a longitudinal DC-EEG study;* M Bangert & E O Altenmüller (2003).

As you stand, looking out to sea, your inner legend appears beside you. He stands next to you, strong. He wants you to know **he's always been inside you. He's part of *you*.**

You feel his strength and groundedness. Being with him makes you feel safe, protected and loved.

He gives you a gift. You open it and find parts of who you are that you'd forgotten.

You reclaim all these parts of you, placing them back in your heart one by one as new memories, ones where you acted as a man of honour and integrity.

Self-love pours back into you.

From this moment forward, you love and respect yourself. You respect every life around you as equally valuable and precious.

In your heart, you're now integrated back to wholeness.

You and The Legend are one in the same man. Connecting fully to this part of you will give you access to all the power, courage, truth and wisdom that lies within you, allowing your life to blossom into one of freedom and true honour.

3

FOR THE LOVE OF SEX

---

(12) "So tell me [insert name of un-suspecting date], how do you make love?"

What a fantastic first-date question. Okay, maybe not the *first* date. But think about it.

THE WAY YOU MAKE LOVE IS THE WAY YOU LIVE YOUR LIFE.

Rushed, smooth, selfless, selfish, seeking pleasure, seeking pain – it's a direct mirror to how we go about our lives. So, personally, I'll be asking this question *before* the first date! Of course I'll deliver it with a good dose of flirty banter, but the answer is going to tell me so much about a person, right from the start.

I'm no sex expert, but I do know that sex is the life force behind every-thing we do. It's the most beautiful, natural exchange of synthetic energy and should be celebrated, not demonised. Human beings are hardwired to need sexual connection. There is no shame in being one of those hu-mans!

I'd be crazy to write a book about love and tip-toe around the topic of sex. Or, worse still, avoid it altogether. So we're not doing that. Instead, we're hitting it hard on (pun intended).

(13) What is the difference between fucking and making love?

I'm going to leave it to you to find your own answer to this question. For me, when you're tackling sex like a step-by-step process to reach the end climax, you're fucking. You're in your head, thinking about the *performance*, about making your partner come, about making sure *you* come. I get it. There is so much pressure to 'do' and achieve things in life, and it's the same in the bedroom. Yet, the feel-good moment upon crossing the finish line is just that – a moment. The thing with moments? They pass. And when they do, you often realise it wasn't as good as you imagined, and you're miles away from who and where you wanted to be in the first place, completely disconnected. Remember our dive into the perils of pursuing the "next best thing"? Seeing the parallel to life?

While you're laser-focused on performing your signature, 3-step cha-cha-cha to make your partner come, you're totally tuned out of the moment *with* them, turning sex into a 'doing' act. And trust me, no woman wants to feel like she's being 'done to'. In fact, it's a huge turn off. She feels the disconnect so strongly that it completely offsets any pleasure you *do* give her. I mean, let's be honest, fucking or going down on someone like they're a to-do list stuck to your fridge among the holiday magnets is hardly *romantic*, right? Even if it's a *really nice to-do list*. I've been with someone who made me come every time. It was the most unfulfilling, soulless sex. You come? Then what, you come again? Then what? Like life, sex should be about the journey, not the destination (cliché, I know, but true).

So, if that's fucking, what's making love?

It's different, very different. Making love requires you to completely abandon any anxiety around having to 'perform' or achieve any kind of result. It requires you to be fully present. Focus on creating a string of beautiful, unpredictable moments. Moments that make the hairs on the back of your neck stand up. Moments of anticipation. Moments of deep connection and harmony with another person. Don't leapfrog over those moments, you deserve them. They are food for the soul. Take your time with each little sensation. Every kiss. Every touch. Every taste. Every sound.

I've never approached sex like that before. It sounds super uncomfortable.

Intimacy (which can be aptly read as 'into-me-you-see') creates a context that can feel incredibly vulnerable, exposing and bloody terrifying sometimes, especially if you've never made love in this way. I hear you. Those feelings are completely valid. To lay yourself bare and drop into a deeper connection can be really difficult. But if you want to put the soul back into sex, it's absolutely necessary. My advice? Swap judgement (of yourself and your partner) for compassion. Because from vulnerability comes an opportunity to be fully seen and *loved* for who you are. From vulnerability comes beauty.

So be patient and start simple. Start with eye-contact.

(14) I've slept with plenty of women and never had any complaints, so I can't be doing that badly?!

Nowadays, sleeping around is seen as some kind of conquest, a KPI of manhood even! Staring deeply into the eyes of this week's one night stand for too long would be a bit of a weird move, I'll admit. 'Soul connection' would be a bit of a stretch. Sure, sometimes we *need* to experiment and explore in order to know our likes, dislikes, wants and needs. There is absolutely no shame in doing so. That is how we learn. Don't chastise yourself for that. However, you cannot possibly live fully and 'Love the Fuck out of Everything' if you're habitually 'Fucking the Love out of Everything'.

———

25

If you're going to sleep around, I encourage you to do so protected by the armour of knowing your boundaries and who you are inside. Listen to your body's signals, the 'gut feeling' on whether something feels good to you or not. Lean into the things that feel good. Shut down the things that don't. And along the way, don't forget to come up for air and check in with yourself – *"Am I genuinely enjoying this?" "Does this actually feel good?" "Is this a place of connection?"* Guard against getting so distracted by pursuing multiple women that the most fulfilling sexual experiences completely pass you by, and you miss out on the purpose-driven life you're worthy of.

(15) Why can't I seem to separate pain and pleasure anymore?

Sex can be a place of either healing or re-traumatising. Society presents a rigid dichotomy between pain and pleasure, between calm and chaos, between fucking and making love. This is bullshit. Reality is not so black and white. Whilst we've established that fucking and making love are two distinct ingredients, perhaps utopia requires mixing these two ingredients together? Today's media heavily glamourises the pain element of sex (Exhibit A: '50 Shades of Grey'),[9] with portrayals of sex as a place of mutual trust and equal power exchange being far less popular in the box office. We have to question why this is. As a society, we are chasing the version we see on our screens, thinking that's how great sex is meant to look. We've convinced ourselves that this version of sex is the dream, but completely failed to recognise that we're dreaming of a place rooted in pain and trauma. Chasing that dream unarmed by a strong sense of self is when we get hurt, used and abused.

I want to challenge that dream. Many, myself included, have at some point sought pain in our sex lives, as a form of disconnect. Why? Because we can disguise the reliving of our trauma as 'a good fucking',

---

9   *50 Shades of Grey*, E. L. James.

and doing so seems to offer a solid distraction when life gets heavy. I know I'm not alone in having gone through times when I've felt so numb and disconnected, that seeking pain and pleasure in sex seemed to be the only way to feel something, *anything*. I wasn't listening to what my body was telling me. I was fucking myself over. In doing so, I spiralled far from who I was and the love I wanted. I was so focused on performing and being what the other person wanted me to be that I wasn't in the moment. I completely lost out on the beauty. You deserve more than that.

Like I was, maybe you're seeking pain because you *need* to relive your trauma in order to move past it and learn. That is okay. Do not judge yourself for that. Because it's through our bodies that we heal. For me, the combination of that spiral and giving birth to my second child taught me so much. It was the catalyst for the most life-changing growth and healing. When I started to listen to my body and learned to love and accept myself, everything changed. Even the pain.

I learned that sex doesn't need to be that way. You can choose pleasure over disconnect and pain. You can choose pleasure just once, sometimes, or *every fucking time*. Let the bedroom be a place of connection and healing, not a place of chaos and retraumatising. Of course, if you need to relive your trauma in order to move past it, do that. But don't fuck yourself over in the process. Remember, if you want to live a life of purpose, eventually you need to get on and move the fuck past it. If you don't, you're clipping your own wings. You will be consistently pulled back if you *keep* choosing to relive that pain. Love the fuck out of yourself, enough to give in to the pleasure instead.

FANTASIES

(16) Should I feel guilty for having a fantasy?

___

Fantasies. Let's talk about them. Having a fantasy is so important. We need the power of the present *and* the power of a fantasy. After all, fantasies are fun and life is meant to be enjoyed! If the fantasy you're imagining makes you feel good, why is that so wrong? Sometimes we need that, especially when reality is not serving our soul anymore and life gets really...*lifey.*

Enjoy the fantasy, but proceed with caution. Don't miss out on reality.

The problem comes when we start feeling resentful or disappointed by the reality of our life, the person we're with, the sex we're having, ourselves...because none of it lives up to the fantasy we imagined. Quite often, fantasy is a mirror for what we feel we're lacking within ourselves.

I'll give you an example. After my divorce, I began falling for a charismatic, entrepreneurial man I'd never met. He wasn't real. I got catfished. I had built a fantasy in my mind of who this person was and who we'd become together. I could have felt humiliated by the whole situation, sure. But I switched my perspective on it. I realised that my fantasy of this person was a mirror to everything I wanted to be. Rather than sit around playing a small violin, wallowing in my own self-pity, I decided to focus on how the experience served me. I decided to reclaim the determined, entrepreneurial go-getter I was before getting married. Once I switched to viewing this experience as a gift that helped me reclaim parts of myself I'd lost along the way, I'd never felt more empowered or free in my life. I thank that man for holding up the mirror I needed. I thank him for shocking me into taking action and becoming the Legend I'd always wanted to be.

(17) Cool, but what about sexual fantasies?

Perhaps the biggest fantasy that plagues our psyches is porn. One big performance, it showcases a well-orchestrated scene brought to life by paid actors, producers, camera crew and makeup artists. Remind me when last you had a team offering you creative direction in the sheets? Didn't think so. Besides, when you're in the moment, you don't need all that anyway.

Porn sells us the lie that having a big dick and putting in a solid performance makes you a great lover. Unfortunately, they've forgotten to caveat this with the truth that women don't give a flying fuck about your size or performance, especially when what you have with them is true intimacy. But you're not to blame for believing that. Maybe you've even had wounded women shame you around these issues. For many men, the little boy they once were had nowhere else to go with his questions about sex. Mum and Dad probably weren't the type to talk openly about it, so he learned through porn, because where else is there? Porn taught him how to fuck. But he thought it also taught him what women want. He thought it taught him how to *make love*. Here I go with the myth-busting again...

Being fucked like you're drilling for oil is *not* what a woman wants. The large majority of genuine women want you to connect with them, listen to them, hold a space for emotional exchange. Sit with your partner's and your own emotions, the tears, the anger, all of it. Confronting and embracing that emotion is the strongest, most masculine thing you can do. And until you do, you're still just that misguided little boy, running around fucking the love out of everything. Successful men have mastered the art of breathing life into the bedroom by creating room for this deeper connection, and they enjoy the most breath-taking sex because of it.

Remember, you're armed with the security of knowing that you are worth more than simply how you perform in the sack. Once you really *go there* emotionally, you'll open yourself up to having the most connected, powerful sexual experiences.

(18) I'm on a hamster wheel of porn and empty sex. Is there a way out?

When making love, your brain releases dopamine, endorphins and oxytocin that connects you to the other person. Whilst porn similarly triggers the release of these hormones, it creates an unnatural high that connects you to an experience which is not real.[10]

Porn numbs. Making love ignites.

Empty sex creates stale. Making love creates success.

We're not striving for stale, are we? If your life is more familiar with porn and empty sex than you'd like to admit, that doesn't mean you're damaged. That doesn't mean you need therapy. You just need somewhere safe to heal. Let this book be that first safe place for you. I promise that you are so much more than your muscles and your dick size. You don't need to trade sex, status, or money, because everything you need is already within you. Let sex now be about what you *give*. And the most valuable thing you can give to a woman? True connection, in the moment. Funnily enough, connection like that is just about the only thing in this life that cannot be discarded, no matter how hard we sometimes try!

(19) How do I create connection and break the cycle?

Put distance between yourself, social media and the fake, disconnected world. Instead, learn to play again. Think about how you and your partner used to play as children. Did you enjoy building Lego? Build some flat-pack furniture together. Did your parents always find you making a mess in the kitchen? Attempt a weird and wonderful recipe together.

---

10   *Pornography Addiction and the Brain*; Sustain Recovery

Used to run riot around the garden? Run a new route together. Were you one for making up songs or poems? Write her a love letter. Did you love building blanket forts? Sounds like your next date night is a picnic on the living room floor, underneath a blanket fort. Enjoying playful moments born out of the simplest pleasures is what creates memories and real connection. Allow yourself to play and let your imagination run. Creativity is key with this. Put 'fuck bitches get money' on the back burner and get busy learning how to create magic out of nothing.

(SIXTY)NINE TO FIVE

(20) Should I mix business and pleasure?

There should be more space given to discussions around sex in business books and career coaching. Innately, we are sexual beings with desires. That energy and drive is the most powerful thing about being human – we shouldn't be attempting to suppress it, for fuck's sake!

Surrounding yourself with attractive people and feeling sexual tension with those in your workplace is not, in itself, wrong. It's what you *do* with that tension that differentiates between the master and the amateur.

Capture it, cultivate it, then channel it.

Sexual transmutation is the concept of channelling the build-up of sexual energy into something else.[11] Your ability to channel it into your work and creativity will determine whether you become stunted or successful. Believe me, when redirected into our work, that intense sexual energy can be an absolute *superpower.* The successful don't dampen that superpower. They leverage it to produce something that propels them forward professionally. They respect themselves and the position of power they

11   *What is Sexual Transmutation? How to Transmute Sexual Energy;* Sarah Regan

have when leading others at work, and save acting on it for their personal life. Think and Grow Rich[12] floats the idea that many men don't become successful until after 40 because they fail to harness and redirect their sexual power in this way. In other words, the...*less successful*... camp jump straight into screwing SueFromAccounts.

My views on mixing business and pleasure are poetically captured by the saying "don't shit where you eat". Sleeping with colleagues, especially someone junior to you, is an abuse of power that puts them in a vulnerable position. Taking advantage of that is not only weak, but will stunt your growth (both personal and professional) and create drama in your life. In summary, if you want success, save the drama for TV and put that energy into your work.

---

12   *Think and Grow Rich,* Napoleon Hill (2003).

4

A LOVE LETTER TO YOU, DEAR READER

My reader, my Valentine,

I invite you on a journey to your heart. Sit down, close your eyes and come with me.

Place your hand on your heart.

If you ever get lost, remember to place your hand on your heart and hear these words in your mind.

I love you with all my heart and soul. For I am you, and you are me. Together we are **one**.

Remember; when the nights are cold, when you feel lost and alone – I am always with you.

I believe in your heart. I believe in your love. I believe in **you**.

I want you to know that you are **not** what's **happened to you**. You are not what you have **done** or who you have **been**. Know that, from this moment forward, all is forgiven.

You are loved now.

At every step of your journey, you did what you did because you knew no better. You made your choices because that was all you knew. Imagine all of these memories from your past changing into love. They might change colour. You might even rewrite your story in your mind.

My love, you are a hero in **your** story now. **You are a hero of the heart.**

Please my love, repeat these words to yourself every day:

I LOVE YOU. NOW, TODAY, ALWAYS AND FOREVER. I LOVE YOU WHEN YOU'RE HAPPY, I LOVE YOU WHEN YOU'RE SAD, I LOVE YOU WHEN YOU'RE MAD.

I LOVE **ALL** PARTS OF YOU.

When you don't feel lovable, close your eyes and imagine me holding you. Imagine me holding your hand, putting my hand on your heart. **You deserve** all of the love. **You are love**.

Everything you've experienced has made you **YOU.** You are **perfect**, you are **enough**, you are **loved**.

All my love, forever and always.

PART 2

PART 2

Part 1 was for introspection. We looked at the *internal* – the love you give yourself: the man you were, the man you are and the man you aspire to be.

In Part 2, we're switching gears, because love is not insular. It's not something that exists in a vacuum and only affects us. Like oxygen, love is a life force that impacts everyone and everything in our lives. So, let's turn our attention to external love – love *outside* of ourselves.

We will answer some common questions around relationships beyond the dating stage, exes, marriage and divorce. And, of course, *woman-kind*.

Before we dig in, I am going to set the tone of this second half by offering some food for thought in the form of re-imagining the "love and obey" wedding vow. Vowing to obey your partner resembles signing up to a lifelong sentence of possession and control. Two people don't need to 'obey' one another in order to have a fulfilling marriage. Instead, they need to stay true to their own beliefs whilst respecting the other's perspective, listening with an open heart and holding a judgement-free space for each other. For *that* is where love overflows. Wedding vows set an intention for the relationship, not just the wedding day. With this in mind, what if we spin the script to resemble a marital commitment characterised by freedom instead?

"…~~I vow to love and obey~~…"

"I vow to give you the freedom to be who you are in this world.

May I be a source of love.

May our home be a place of happiness for all who enter it; a place for music and laughter, a place for peace and love.

May I be a powerful force behind you, to help you create, love and live every expression of who you are.

I will rise with you not only in our light, but when darkness falls I will have your back.

I will share with you deeper experiences and soul connection like you've never had before.

I vow to be the home you go to; to give you more than my arms, but my forgiveness, compassion and loyalty too.

May those around us be constantly enriched by the beauty of our love.

I love you."

Does this rewrite make sense to you? Does it make you feel uneasy? Does it provoke something in you that you didn't think it would?

Like I said, food for thought.

5

FOR THE LOVE OF US

These next two chapters are going to tackle relationships, breakups and everything in between. We're talking about where you think (or once thought) you've found your 'soulmate'. Situations where you're deeply intertwined with another person, for better or worse. Where, rightly or wrongly, you couldn't imagine your life without them.

We'll start with the good stuff first. Relationships are not just the combination of two individuals. They are also the energy those individuals create together. Seeing relationships as energy will help you to understand that you will create something different with your partner each time, depending on the energy you both put in.

So, let's explore some questions I've helped many clients work through, around how to be in a healthy, fulfilling relationship and *maintain* that fulfilment. How to *enjoy* it, pour into it, give to it in every way you can, and celebrate that beautiful connection you're blessed to have with another soul, the person that 'just gets you'.

(21) What's the secret recipe for being in a successful relationship?

We're diving straight in with the big, juicy question. There ain't no idiot-proof user guide for long-lasting, happy relationships. But you, dear reader, are lucky enough to have stumbled on my method for experiencing genuine fulfilment in those connections, taking one day at a time. It goes a little something like this:

01	02	03	04
Be open with yourself	Be open & honest with your partner	Loose attachment to the outcome	The response informs your next steps

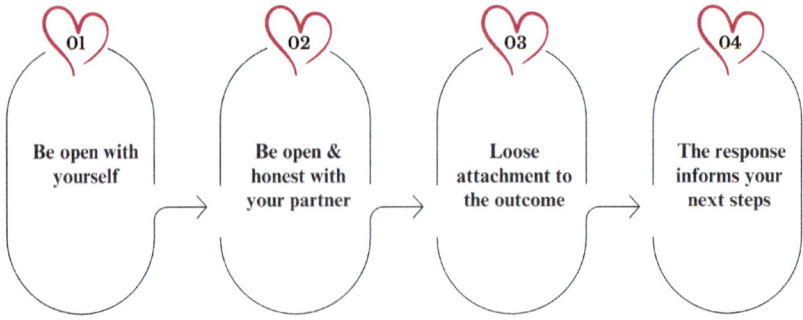

Step 1: Be open with yourself

First off, those slick little rose-tinted glasses? Bin them. Swap them for holding a magnifying glass up to what's *really* going on with *you*. What's happening in your life, in your head? Are there any internal conflicts that perhaps you need to work through?

Work on feeling *pride* when you look in the mirror. Feeling proud of the person you're *being* (note that this is not the same thing as feeling proud of the *things* you're *doing*) is a self-respect that no lover, friend or enemy can take from you. And *that's* your starting point when it comes to 'nailing' any relationship – it starts within you...hardly a shock at this point in the book though, right?!

Step 2: Be open and honest with your partner

A vast majority of men find it incredibly difficult to speak their truth with their partners. Often, they fear that their unfiltered, blunt honesty will "come out wrong" or be misinterpreted and "taken the wrong way". I want to address this head-on and say: that fear is valid! But unfortunately, mate, you still *need* to speak your truth and have those conversations. Running from it will rob you of the *fresh, cold pint at the end of a long, hot day* kind of life, and deliver you a *flat, tepid and tinny* experience instead. No one wants that.

So speak to your partner with full openness and honesty. Where there are things bothering you in the relationship, think about what you or your partner may need from those conversations before going into them. For example, is there simply a need to be heard? Often, men default to jumping straight into Fix-It Mode and throw out 301 solutions to her problem. I'll let you in on a secret. *A lot* of the time, women don't want you to do anything whatsoever, let alone fix it. They just want you to be present and *listen*. That's it. Just listen. So keep this in mind and *ask* her what support she needs most from you in that moment.

And vice versa. If you speak your truth and your partner responds with volatility, defensiveness, the kitchen sink and everything but a willing-ness to *listen*, I will ditch the sugar-coating and make the upfront sug-gestion that she's not right for you. While it might not be what you want to hear, those reactions are indicative of a relationship based on fear, rather than true intimacy. When the building blocks are fear, people cannot be openly truthful with each other. This is the birthplace for in-fidelity, dishonesty, broken trust and shaky foundations that struggle to withstand the shit life inevitably throws at us.

So, in a bid to channel the *cold pint* kind of connection you deserve, con-front those uncomfortable conversations by putting honesty, empathy, kindness and a willingness to listen on the table. Walsch sums it up best when he says that "romance demands a hero's heart. Romantic love is a quest...a noble pursuit and a challenging path. To approach it lightly is to not approach it at all."[13]

Step 3: Lose attachment to the outcome

Oftentimes, we struggle to be honest in life, and especially in our rela-tionships. This is not for lack of trying or *wanting* to lie. Rather, we're

---

13   *Conversations with God;* Neale Donald Walsch (2006).

too caught up in trying to control the outcome or predict the other person's reaction to our honesty. Frankly, this is utterly useless. Being attached to particular outcomes of conversations, relationships and situations doesn't serve us in any way. It just puts our self-doubt on steroids and wastes our precious time, energy and sanity.

The fact of the matter? You can neither *know* nor *control* how a situation will play out. Regardless of how hard you might try. The sooner you're able to accept that reality, the sooner you can come to a place of authenticity. Let's take a 'worst case scenario'. Say, for example, you share your true feelings with your partner and they react negatively – they shout and scream, get defensive and ultimately end the relationship. That thought might panic you. It might unnerve you. But I challenge you to embrace the fact that you could not have controlled or predicted that reaction either way. That is okay. Because you've stayed true to yourself and been completely authentic.

Step 4: Let the response inform your next move

Rather than squashing or slanting your truth in a bid to control the fallout, shift your mindset to a place where sharing your truth is a given. Share it, then pay close attention to someone's unfiltered *reaction* to that truth, for it will pull the curtains back and expose what your next steps should be.

Don't allow fear of a negative reaction to dissuade you from being honest and cause you to betray your truth. Instead, let that reaction inform how you should respond and move forward. Their reaction will tell you how they value themselves, how they value their attachment to you and the relationship and how they perceive the situation. This information is gold dust, because you will quickly learn whether your values align, and if there is mutual respect and space in that relationship for you to be seen and heard for who you are.

In this way, your partner's response will bring you learnings and clarity as to whether you can stay and work through things, or whether that soul contract has ended and you're better off going separate ways. Your mental energy is far better spent on taking proper note of their response, rather than trying to control outcomes and make sure things turn out "exactly how you pictured" in your fantasy. At the end of the day, the *right* relationship for you and the one worth nurturing will be one where you both respond to one another with heart-centred understanding and compassion.

(22) How do I keep things exciting?

Before I answer, I want to tell you that it's totally normal if you feel like you have *no idea* what you're doing, or 'how' to be in a relationship. Society seems adamant that you "can't love anyone until you love yourself". I call bullshit. We learn relationships by being in them. You absolutely can learn how to love your partner in tandem with continuing to grow and love yourself. There is a lot you can learn from stepping out of your comfort zone, trying things and being in relationships that allow you to make mistakes and understand your truth.

I'll set the scene. You're in a relationship with a partner that you love, trust, laugh with and care about. However, the 'honeymoon phase' has passed and you can feel the infatuation wearing off. You're slowly realising that, yes, her shit stinks too. You still love her deeply, but you're worried about things getting *"too comfortable"* and want to know how to keep things exciting.

CREATE
SACREDNESS &
APPRECIATION

CONNECT &
COMMUNICATE

FOCUS ON WHO
YOU'RE BEING

I'm going to challenge you on that. 'Excitement' isn't what we should be aspiring for. If you want to keep your love strong and your relationship fresh, try striving for: harmony, peace, sacredness and less distraction. How? Don't you worry – I have a handy diagram that will help you pursue this.

(a) Create sacredness and appreciation in the relationship

Perhaps my most prominent piece of advice when it comes to main-taining a connection of pure joy is to make the relationship a place of sacredness, where there is nothing but admiration and appreciation for the person you share that connection with.

Create a routine with your partner – something you do *together,* every single day. Given how impressionable our subconscious is when we wake up in the morning, my preference would be a morning ritual, to set the tone for the day ahead. Whichever time of day works for you, the point is to set aside a designated time together, during which you share gratitude for each other and the fact that, today, your partner is by your side and chose you. This is not meant to be a grand gesture or 'big deal'. It's a quiet, shared and – *intentional* – moment.

This will look different for every couple, as every connection is entirely unique. However you go about it, the key ingredient is *eye contact*. Perhaps you could start with an 'eye-contact cuppa' first-thing every morning, during which you simply sit in silence over a cup of tea, still and peaceful, looking with admiration and gratitude into each other's eyes. How beautiful, to do that with another soul.

Alongside implementing a daily ritual, elevating 'excitement' in a relationship can also come from making the bedroom a sacred space, and approaching making love as an honour. During sex, take your time to worship each other's bodies, admire every sensation and the beauty of your shared, intimate connection. Cherish the sharing of an uninterrupted moment with the person closest to you.

(b) Focus on who you're *being*, not what you're doing

Another one of the industry's 'top tips' when it comes to getting relationships *all figured out* is The Five Love Languages; the brainchild of Dr. Gary Chapman.[14] To summarise very broadly, the theory suggests that people express and receive love in one or more of the following languages; quality time, words of affirmation (compliments and reassurance, for instance), gifts, acts of service and physical touch. These can be briefly summarised like so:

---

14   *The Five Love Languages: How to Express Heartfelt Commitment to Your Mate,* Dr. Gary Chapman (1992).

QUALITY TIME	WORDS OF AFFIRMATION	GIFT	ACTS OF SERVICE	PHYSICAL TOUCH
Give your partner undivided attention whilst you're together.	Compliment or encourage your partner, tell them the positive traits you love about them, or even speak words of forgiveness.	Gifts symbolise that you thought about your partner. Whether they're purchased, found or made, the thought matters more than the cost.	Seek to please them by serving them and doing things they'd like you to do.	Touch does not always need to be sexual in nature or intent. It can be holding hands, kissing or back rubs too.
• Go home for dinner together • Be protective of your time together • Give them undistracted attention when they talk.	• Tell them why you're proud of them • Compliment them in front of others • Say you're sorry • Tell them your intimate thoughts & feelings	• Flowers • Small surprise gifts • Buy their favourite magazine	• Do one of your partner's household chores • Do tasks around the house • Groom yourself in preparing for time together	• Hold your partner when they're upset • Spend more time being affectionate • Comb their hair

15

Chapman's Love Languages provide a helpful starting point when it comes to not only understanding how to 'succeed' in our relationship, but also being aware of which childhood deficits our love languages answer. For example, if your partner lights up when you surprise them with a thoughtful gift, that doesn't make them materialistic. Perhaps they grew up never having the things their friends had? Understanding the itch being scratched is crucial to nurturing your partner and helping heal any residual wounds.

However, I believe a key warning is missing. Proceed with caution.

Neatly tucking your partner away into their designated love language box and thinking you've got it all figured out might work if you want to stay stagnant in a mediocre, relatively boring relationship. However, we started this section asking how to keep things exciting – so the fact

15   *The Five Love Languages, A summary of Dr. Gary Chapman's principles;* http://damacleod.com/index_files/handouts/Five%20Love%20Languages%20Summary.pdf

you're still reading tells me you want more than plain, old *average*. No two days are guaranteed. Nor is the love you have or the person you're with. That is exciting in itself! So if you love life with your partner and want to keep them around: stop assuming and start asking questions.

Whilst flowers may light her up today, she may need you to simply tell her that you're proud of her tomorrow. Humans ebb and flow like water, ever changing depending on anything from our circumstances to the energy we're around on a particular day. Don't oversimplify your partner's 'acts of service' love language as yet another tick-box exercise (you already got a slap on the wrist for the to-do lists in Chapter 2)! Instead, embrace child-like curiosity. Stay inquisitive. Check in with her, *daily.*

Where's your head at, today?

What would your perfect day look like?

What emotions are coming up for you?

What would your perfect support system for today be?

Be a man who is able to ask questions. Be a man who can hear the answers without getting defensive. Be a man who thanks their partner for honesty and holds a non-judgemental space for open communication. Be a man who seeks to truly understand his partner and what is important to them. Be love.

If you're checking in with your partner by asking the above questions, you're halfway there. The next half of the journey requires you to listen to the answers *actively.* Don't fall into the trap of robotically nodding along and blindly agreeing to everything they say. They will pick up that you're just paying them lip service, which is unattractive in itself. Your listening should be vocal. Notice your partner's tone of voice and body language as they talk, then follow up with questions that help you to fully understand where they're coming from and what they need.

A simple *"Is this what you meant when you said...?"* will change your life. Not only will it help you, but your partner will feel truly heard, valued and understood.

Vocal listening is an extremely attractive masculine trait. Don't squash that. You don't have to agree with everything your partner says, but listen to their viewpoint openly, with your own set of opinions too. Two conflicting sets of opinions *can* co-exist. You *can* disagree with each other and still treat each other with love and respect. Keep that at the forefront of your mind.

So, stop overthinking about what you could be *doing* to keep things exciting. To keep the relationship fresh, put your energy into *being* kind, inquisitive, actively engaged in what she says and does, respectful, loving, supportive and…fun. You will excite her and bring such a light energy to your relationship, simply by *being* that presence in her life.

(c) Connect and communicate

Relationships fail altogether over a lack of connection, forget being "unexcited". Whilst people try to blame a myriad of crazy and creative stories to explain why their relationship ended, none of the stories are ever the root cause. It's a lack of connection.

Every. Fucking. Time.

Many of us lose sight of this. We get easily wrapped up in creating drama, talking to everyone *but* our partner about the good, bad and ugly parts of our relationship, then seem surprised when we start feeling a tangible distance in the relationship. That void is the disconnect that begins when you stop having open, honest conversations with your partner in a safe space. Before we know it, this quickly snowballs into a lack of transparency, empathy and intimacy ('into-me-you-see', remember).

Building the 'excitement' that comes from intimacy is all about having hard, raw conversations with your partner about anything and everything. This includes talking openly and candidly about sex. Fostering a nurturing yet transparent dialogue will not just keep your relationship from becoming stale, it will make it blossom. Because suddenly, both parties can bring their 'full selves' into the relationship, rather than simply existing to please the other. And the thing about that true authenticity? It's fun. It's real. It's exciting as fuck.

(23) Why don't my relationships ever last longer than one year?

If you feel like you're on some kind of 'annual subscription' to relationships, automatically renewing with the latest model after one year, this one's for you.

I'm going to preface my answer to this question with a big, fat caveat: a relationship can be a success whether it lasts two days, two years or a lifetime! If you moved through that relationship with kindness, integrity, honesty and a pure heart, it was a success. We should not be using longevity as our only measure of success in relationships. Now, back to business.

Reason 1 – Playing a character

When we meet someone and decide we like them, we all have an innate desire to impress them, to be liked back. Human nature. So, we stay on our best behaviour and go to great lengths to showcase the best *version* of ourselves. In doing so, we unconsciously betray ourselves by selling a lie. Our new partner falls for a version of us that is not who we really are. Fast forward one or two years and, inevitably, that mask begins to

---

drop. You and your partner start to uncover what's really under the bonnet. Lo and behold, predictable lines like *"you've changed"* and *"you're just not the person I fell in love with"* start being thrown around. Sound familiar?

I'll give you a relatable example. You're in the early stages of dating a girl you really like and decide to 'play it cool'. If that 'cool' character is not really who you are, what happens when you drop the act a few months later and want to be told you're loved, or want someone to cook a warm meal for you, or want your shoulders rubbed after a long day? Either, you'll betray yourself by not voicing your desire for these things, and land yourself in an unfulfilling relationship that can't last long-term. Or, if you do voice these desires, you could be asking for more intimacy than your partner is able to give without compromising *their* own happiness in the relationship.

Either way, you've shot yourself in the foot by playing a character in the beginning. Instead, cut the shit and be yourself from the start, so that those you date know exactly what they're getting themselves into. Stay true to your values and what you really want. If these things "scare her off", she wasn't the one for you and you've just freed up a shit tonne of time, which can now be invested in connecting with someone that *is* right for you. You're welcome.

Reason 2 – Avoiding yourself

Relationships can fail early on for another reason that has fuck all to do with the other person, or even the relationship itself. It has everything to do with the fact that you haven't taken the time to deeply connect to the man you are (as described in Chapter 3). In other words, you ain't *feeling* your feelings. Maybe you find yourself unable to 'go deep' and commit to another person without running - *#MrCommitmentIssues*?

You might not realise that the thing making you run is fear. Fear of unpacking your emotions and unravelling, however 'messy' that might be. You're keeping things 'neat and tidy' by running away, to avoid having to unpack those emotions. Unfortunately, my friend, both science and I are here to tell you that, eventually, the feelings catch up to you.[16] Which means that, not only have you self-sabotaged your budding new relationship before it even got to the good bit, but you've also been unsuccessful in the attempted burial of your feelings.

If you want a fulfilled life, you can't run forever. Besides, being eternally on the run sounds exhausting. Lundquist recommends that, to save yourself the energy and break this cycle, you need to do what feels most scary: feel the feelings, so you can move on from them.[17] Like physical pain, emotional pain is only ever temporary. So brace yourself for any initial agony that comes from letting those feelings in, and take comfort in knowing that it *will* subside. It will make way for beautiful, deeply-connected relationships with long-haul kinds of people who will be there through your brightest and most broken days. Of course, if you'd rather not, you're in for a long, lonely run on that 'one-year relationship' hamster wheel. Keep the sweatbands handy…

Reason 3 – Expectations

Maybe your own expectations of *#relationshipgoals* are killing the magic that *is* there? Take responsibility for that.

Like many, I allowed expectations to dampen the joy in my past relationships. The idyllic *white-picket-fence, finish-each-other's-sentences* type of relationship was so deeply ingrained in my subconscious. I wanted 'perfect' so badly. When I eventually got the fairy-tale marriage I'd wanted, I was only too ready to shout it from the rooftops.

16   Monica Parikh
17   Matt Lundquist, LCSW

However, my expectations of the 'perfect marriage' and need to prove I'd 'made it' were coming from a place of wounding and not feeling loved in the past. I wanted to feel loved so badly, I had created an expectation of my husband to be someone he wasn't. Whilst he'd try his best to fulfil those expectations, that wasn't and never would be his reality. And that was *my* fault, not his, because I'd created an expectation that he was doomed to fall short of from the start. While I only had good intentions, that expectation blindfolded me and left me struggling to find joy in the reality of my marriage, and the man my husband really was. Instead, I tried to mould him into the person my fantasy said he should be. Real talk.

If your relationships keep ending after a short time, perhaps take a moment to put yourself in the hotseat. Question whether your partners keep 'falling short' of expectations you create in your own head. Are you holding them to a standard that is pure fantasy, rather than celebrating the person they are in reality? Are you trying to control or change them to fit society's *#relationshipgoals* mould?

If you're brutally honest with yourself and find that some of the above applies to you, as it did to me in my marriage, then you do not love the person you're with, no matter how much you *think* you do. That is the hard truth. Because love is not possession or control. Love can't be owned or contained. Trying to contain someone and mould them into the outcome we expect is often what destroys the magic and fucks up our relationships.

Stop fucking it up. Start loving.

Choose to love them. Give your partner the freedom to breathe, to be true to who they are, to change, grow and evolve, without expecting any kind of outcome. That freedom is true love.

---

(24) Is my childhood affecting my adult relationships?

The short answer to this question: Yes.

Attachment is a "deep and enduring emotional bond that connects one person to another person across time and space."[18] Building on original research by Bowlby, the 'Strange Situation' experiment conducted by Ainsworth (1973) identified three 'attachment styles':

> *Secure*. Born from a loving bond between parent and child, securely attached individuals demonstrate confidence and form healthy, long-term relationships without fearing abandonment.

> *Anxious*. Coming from having grown up in an environment where intimacy and affection were given inconsistently, anxiously-attached adults often do everything they can to be close to their partner, requiring affection and emotional affinity to feel safe and secure in the relationship.

> *Avoidant*. Rooted in feeling insignificant and accepting that their emotional needs are likely to remain unmet, avoidantly-attached adults often avoid intimate relationships, struggling to express their feelings and understand emotions.[19]

So how does this explain an 'annual subscription' relationship pattern?

Start by comparing your childhood and adult relationships. Do any patterns emerge in the type of women you gravitate towards now, versus the type of attention you craved or lacked as a child? For instance, did you grow up feeling like you had to work hard for love? If so, you may find yourself enjoying 'the chase' or 'wanting what you can't have' as an

---

18   Ainsworth, 1973; Bowlby, 1969
19   https://www.attachmentproject.com/attachment-style-and-breakup/

adult. Or perhaps you find yourself pursuing those who are the opposite to you – think about what you may be trying to repair? Were you smothered and not given much space as a child? That may explain why you're unsure how to set healthy boundaries with partners and find yourself running from intimacy as an adult.

I don't shed light on this to label you or make you wrong. Instead, awareness of the role your childhood attachment style plays in creating patterns in adulthood can help you to rectify any unhealthy relationship dynamics or repeated patterns you're falling prey to. It will also arm you with the ability to distinguish between 'trauma bonding' versus securely-attached love when choosing a partner. The key here is *awareness*. When you're unaware, you're just going through the motions like you're in a video game, where your present is being controlled by your past.

When you're aware and armed with an understanding of attachment styles, *you're* the one in control of your video game, because you can make conscious choices to break old cycles and be smart about the type of partner that will fulfil you, rather than reopen old wounds. Pick the woman with a heart, mind and values that are coherent with yours, for *there* lies the potential for things to blossom into secure, long-lasting connection. And the one that's unable to step up as the partner you need, due to both of your childhood attachments? Maybe she's best kept as a friend.

So the next time you're faced with choosing a partner, ask yourself:

If I completely removed all sexual attraction to the person in front of me, what about them would I still be drawn to?

This one question is a shortcut exercise to move your life's video game controller out of your past's hands and into your own.

6

FOR THE LOVE OF EXES

---

(25) Should I stay or should I go?

I want to acknowledge a space many of us have been in, when we find our-selves in limbo, pondering this type of question or feeling like we're living our relationship with one foot out the door. I'm talking about the point where you no longer feel fully present in the relationship. It feels like you're just going through the motions but your heart isn't in it anymore. You wouldn't be the first person to reach that point. While this is not a unique crossroads, it confronts you with the decision of whether to stay or leave, and the diffi-culty of that question shouldn't be diminished. This is roughly the point at which all those societal voices and self-doubts start creeping in:

I don't want that time to be wasted

I don't want to hurt her

The good times are so good, are the bad times really that bad?

But she hasn't specifically done *anything wrong?*

I'm not sure I'll ever find someone else.

What will our friends and family think?

What about the future we promised each other?

Was it all one big lie?

I can't double back after I told everyone she was the one…

It can be really difficult to find clarity amongst the noise of all these questions running around your head. It's easy to betray ourselves by entering into a relationship that we know isn't right, or staying longer than we should because we're unclear on the next steps we should take. But that's okay. That 'grey area' is part of life. Decision-making is never black and white. Overthinking and expecting to be sure of the 'right' decision before you make it is delusional in a world where perfect decisions only exist in hindsight. That is not living.

If you're searching for clarity, try giving some thought to these types of questions instead:

> How does she make you feel when you're with her?

> How do you feel when she leaves, after spending time together?

> Can you open up to her about your feelings without being made 'wrong'?

> What is she adding to your life, besides sex?

> Is she creating more chaos or more peace in your life?

However you answer the above questions, the decision on whether to stay or go is totally yours to make. I can't (and won't) attempt to tell you what you should do. However, I will say that breaking up shouldn't be done in a state of chaos or simply because you think you'll "feel better" or "get something" from your newfound singledom. That will only create more chaos.

If you're going to end your relationship, my best advice is to come to that decision based on your core beliefs (rather than a desired outcome) and do so when you're in a state of peace, with a clear head and knowledge that, as a result, nothing will change. Because you will still be the person you are, they will still be who they are, and everything you need to move through this is already within you.

If you choose to stay, I want you to grow up and shift your internal monologue. Quit the negativity, fixation on her faults and being preoccupied by external factors such as others' opinions. Instead, make an active choice to honour, love and be kind to her. Amplify the things that are good about her. Shine a light on the things you respect about her. Put your soul connection centre-stage and focus on making that connection as bright, sacred and expansive as it can be. If you look at yourself in the mirror and can truly say that you don't have it in you to make this shift in mentality and behaviour, to make the choice to honour everything about her, it is unfair on both yourself and her to continue the relationship. You need to love and leave her. It's time to go.

(26) I can't forgive my ex for the pain they caused me and the time they wasted.

No matter how much someone might have hurt you, or how painful a breakup may have been, I strongly believe that no time is ever 'wasted'. Time is the most precious gift in life. If you spent time exchanging energy with someone, and did so with an open, pure heart, that time was beautiful, whether or not the relationship ended in the way you expected it to.

You will never find peace and harmony in your life if you continue punishing yourself by viewing that time as wasted. *Look* for the beauty in the time you spent together. The only way you can do that is by swapping the victimhood for deep compassion, for your ex and yourself.

What matters now is how you recalibrate and conduct yourself moving forward, not the time that you think was 'wasted'. Pour your energy into emerging from the fragmentation as a man of honour, integrity, and respect. That takes true, undeniable strength.

Casting your ex as a villain and harbouring a 'you versus me' mentality serves no one, least of all you. It will be a huge turnoff to potential new matches, at best. At worst, it will fuck up your joy and keep you stuck in bitterness and resentment. To get yourself un-stuck, take a walk in your ex's shoes and put in the work to understand their perspective, their circumstances, their context and why they created their reality. Once you're able to appreciate where they may have been coming from, send them love and let it go, so that you can move on and give yourself the opportunity to find the most illuminating love in future.

Whether your ex decides to continue taunting you, completely alienates you, tries to get back together with you or posts literal shit through your letterbox, you cannot control any of that. Let them get on with it. While they're busy with that, focus on the only thing you *can* control; who you're being. Be a light in a shadowed situation. Be respectful and kind when talking about your past with them, regardless of how much that past may have hurt you.

(27) Why can't I seem to 'get over it' or move on?

One of the biggest obstacles in the way of moving on is what I call 'The Story'. The creative, dramatised story of *why* you two broke up. It's the single, least-helpful feature of a breakup, yet it gets the most attention. When you break up with someone, everyone and their dog wants to know what happened, they want to know the story. Guess what, it's no one's business.

The harsh reality is that most of these people want to know the story simply because they love the drama or it makes them feel better about themselves, not because they're actually invested in your wellbeing.

Don't give them the satisfaction. Re-telling the story will only open the door to the wrong advice and keep you in a constant loop of retraumatising. Instead, keep your story to a small circle of people you trust, who simply listen and hold space for you whilst you let the emotion in, process it and move through it.

"People come into your life for a reason, a season or a lifetime."[20] This line by Chalker has had its fair share of fame and become a hanging decoration in many a downstairs loo. But respectfully, it's bollocks.

Whilst the catchy rhyme sticks in our heads, the love you once had for an ex doesn't simply die with the changing of seasons. Thinking that you'll simply wake up one morning being *"over it"* is mad. Everyone who comes into our lives is there for a lifetime. A shared love or experience with someone will never leave you, no matter how much you might want it to, and how pleasantly or painfully that experience ended. A shared experience with someone in the past shapes the person you are in the present. It is, and always will be, a part of you.

Even the rings exchanged in marriage demonstrate this idea. The circular shape symbolises the eternality of truth and love..."that which has no beginning and no end."[21] When you break up, the love still exists, it just exists within a timeline. You can choose how to remember that love and the space you give it. You can choose to heal by remembering your ex giving you kindness, love and security for a time. Or you can remain in turmoil by choosing to remember them being manipulative, threatening or deceitful. Both memories may exist. Neither is wrong. But it's up to you to choose how you hold those memories. Just know that holding onto the negative version for long enough can make you physically sick. So choose wisely – the version of the past you hold onto will be the

20   *Reason, Season and a Lifetime*; Brian A. 'Drew' Chalker (2000).
21   *Conversations with God;* Neale Donald Walsch (2006).

version that controls your present and your future. Maybe you can't 'get over it' or move on because you're clinging to the turmoil?

(28) *How* do I move on?

Frame of Mind

I appreciate that trying to reframe your innermost thoughts and feelings about your ex into something loosely resembling positivity is...*much*... easier said than done. If you can manage nothing else, simply cherish the lessons they taught you and thank them for letting you go, for giving you space. No, I don't mean space to meet someone new. I mean space to fall back in love with the fearless, confident and authentic person you've been neglecting. The person you've been all along. Fall back in love with *you*.

This isn't just wishy-washy, spiritual speak. Research by Parikh observed that securely attached people use breakups as an opportunity to establish what they want in their next relationship. They understand that "not currently being in a relationship isn't reflective of being unworthy of one."[22] The lesson? Love the fuck out of yourself enough to choose positivity and give yourself the permission to blossom and outgrow your ex. That is okay.

Front-row seats

By *outgrowing* your ex, I don't mean kicking them to the curb or denying how deeply you once loved them. You don't have to go through life pretending they don't exist. Society likes to promote an all or nothing approach here, but it doesn't need to be that way.

---

22   *Your Attachment Style Can Impact How You Handle a Breakup;* Nikhita Mahtani (2019).

Imagine your life like a theatre. You're on stage. Your closest, most trusted circle of people get front row seats to the intimate details of your life. To move on from an ex in a healthy way means to simply move them out of the front row seats, with the utmost respect. You're not pretending they never even had a ticket to the show, but they no longer have the privilege of being in your front row. Instead, you can move them somewhere in the middle, where you maintain an amicable friendship. Or you can move them right to the back, where their view of your life is limited, they can't throw orange peels or get close enough to hurt you, and you have the distance you need to heal.

Regardless of their new seat, the point here is that you don't have to cut people from your life completely in order to get on with the show. You can cherish the good in what you had with them, with peace of mind that your front row is reserved only for connections with people that put wind in your sails and don't hold you back from reaching your full potential.

Flirt with your hobbies and passions

Continuing the theatre metaphor, my third ingredient for moving on in a healthy way is giving your hobbies and passions a backstage pass. This could be anything from playing an instrument, enjoying sport, hanging out with family, painting, taking photos, building stuff, *breaking* stuff...

Get up close and personal with the things that make you 'you', the things that used to light you up as a kid. If you don't know what those things are, now is the perfect opportunity to dedicate time and energy to discovering and pursuing them, rather than pursuing a new relationship. Get off your phone and get out there. There's something for everyone and even the act of *trying* to figure out what you like will have you vibrating high.

(29) I'm terrified of getting hurt again!

Amen. That fear makes you human – it was actually a very smart survival tactic, once upon a time in our evolution. If the potential to get hurt didn't scare us humans, we'd have gone extinct long ago.

That fear is not a mistake. It's completely justified and exists for all the right reasons. I don't want you to squash it. Instead, Deida sums it up beautifully: *"Own your fear, and lean just beyond it. In every aspect of your life. Starting now."*[23] Embracing this lesson will propel you forwards with more momentum than you can see coming. I promise you that, deep down, we're all scared. Those who triumph are the ones that embrace the fear. They use it as the siren that sounds when they're outside of their comfort zone and doing something right! Be courageous enough to sound that siren and "trust love one more time".[24]

The warrior of the heart always chooses love, because choosing love means choosing freedom. If you give in to the fear, you're choosing regret, control and restriction of your body, heart and mind. You are not free. You are keeping your body locked in its' 'fight, flight or freeze' trauma response. Being courageous enough to choose love will ground you, reset your heart back to its natural rhythm and, ultimately, heal you. If that scares you, do it scared.

23   *The Way of the Superior Man*; David Deida (2004).
24   Maya Angelou.

DIVORCE

I'm giving the topic of divorce its own space, amidst our discussion of break-ups, for it has a gravitas and impact that stretches further and deeper than other break-ups.

Before going any further, it is vital to acknowledge that our feelings and opinions around the subject of marriage and divorce are the product of our circumstances, childhood, history and experiences. I encourage you to bear that in mind when reading my take on it, and perhaps reflect on how elements of your own past dictate your thoughts on the topic, without you realising. Rather than blindly adopting the opinion society told you was 'right', I urge you to regain control by exploring and absorbing different perspectives, then re-formulating your own opinion with full recognition of the blocks it is built on.

Having been through my own divorce, I'm yet to come to a definitive conclusion on the topic. I believe there is merit in both continuing and ending a marriage. I chose one side of the coin and divorced, whilst my parents chose the other and stayed married, for better or worse. Through my childhood eyes, the 'worse' certainly felt more prevalent than the 'better'. I witnessed years of unhappiness, infidelity and depression, that ultimately seemed more damaging than separation would've been. I used to wish my parents would divorce, just so they'd be happy (an oversimplification I know, but humour my childhood naivety). I don't doubt this played into the later decision-making around my own marriage.

Perhaps it is not as black and white as *Marriage = Good. Divorce = Bad.* Why should we need to believe in *either* marriage *or* divorce? Can you be 'for' marriage *and* 'for' divorce, at the same time? If you can, that's where I fit.

Despite being a divorcee, I still very much believe in the beauty and sanctity of marriage. So much good can come from committing to share your life, soul, home and future with another person in that way. After all, there's a reason why the concept of marriage has spanned continents, cultures and generations.

In the same breath, I don't think longevity should be the marker of 'success' in marriage any more than leaving should be the marker 'failure'. Isn't it more of a failure to stay miserable, unhappy and restricted in a marriage where you can't be yourself or reach your potential?

What I *do* promote is staying true to yourself, whichever outcome is right for you. I believe that it is one of the biggest acts of courage and self-love to leave a marriage that has run its course and is no longer right for you. In no way does this trivialise just how hard and painful divorce is. It can be one of the toughest experiences for both the couple and any children involved. If you let it, it can land you staring trauma, poverty and fear in the face for the rest of your life. BUT, only if you let it!

The strategy to avoid letting it?

(1)

Stay in your integrity, your 'inner legend'. Even after the fact.

When all is said and done, stay in your masculine energy and look after your ex-wife (weren't expecting me to throw that in, were you)! As hard as that might be, it's the right thing to do. Don't disregard her, threaten her stability or try to harm or punish her in any way (financially, physically or emotionally). If you get involved in fanning flames or fuelling drama, the only ones you'll hurt in the end will be you and any children you have together. Your children will feel that instability and lack of love deeply.

Whilst you may not want to be friends with your ex-wife, put your ego aside. It is masculinity in its most primal form to look after, protect and provide for those who depend on you. Embrace that masculinity, for your children's sake.

Avoid getting trapped in bitterness or resentment by taking responsibility for the part *you* played in creating the situation. Regardless of how innocent you think you are, you *will* have played a part in co-creating whatever transpired. Take a step back and ask yourself:

> *How do I want to be remembered at the end of this?*
>
> *How do I want my children to remember me in this season?*
>
> *What will my children think of me when they're adults and see the situation for exactly what it is?*

Don't be the villain in your children's story. Rather than casting yourself as the main character in a twelve-part drama about the petty ins and outs of your divorce, dedicate yourself to being an example of a humble, chivalrous, authentic man. Show your children that, regardless of 'The Story', you will do the right thing by them and their mother and make sure they're all looked after. *That* is a real differentiator. *That* is a legend.

What's more? Any future women you meet will see you behaving as a man who is mature and has unrelenting respect for women (regardless of his own victimhood), a man who protects his family and doesn't shy away from his responsibilities – an *attractive, masculine man.*

(2)

Be selective about your circle. For the first two years following a divorce, research has shown that we revert back to our childhood attachment style. In other words, this is a time when we are incredibly vulnerable to a lot of our ghosts and trauma re-emerging from the childhood closet. Therefore, in this season, it is vital to have the right people surrounding and advising you. Be incredibly picky.

This goes for lawyers, friends and even family. Be wary of those taking advantage or keeping you stuck in anguish because they've got you re-peating The Story over and over. They're only pouring fuel on your fire and, however 'lovingly' they might be going about it or whatever their reasons, they don't have your best interests at heart. Time to welcome them to the back row seats too, maybe? Your pain is not for their enter-tainment. Instead, work through your pain with a coach, therapist, or anyone you trust that can offer you genuine support without any hidden agenda.

(30) How do I know I won't repeat the same thing with the next woman I meet?

The fact of the matter is that, if you haven't done the work to process your pain, heal and re-calibrate as a legend, and you haven't taken time to reflect on the right type of woman for you, you will remarry quickly and the same shit *will* repeat. Perhaps that's why the divorce rate for second marriages is even higher than for the first time around!

When it comes to figuring out the right woman, you need to be having a few tough conversations. If you have children from a previous marriage and your new partner is going to be around them, you should be suggesting that she sit down with your children's mother. It's the respectful thing to do and will help to mitigate any potential tension or competition. Her reaction to this type of suggestion will be a secret weapon in finding out a lot about her character. If she refuses or causes drama over it, perhaps you're getting into bed with a jealous, insecure person? Perhaps you're repeating past mistakes? If she reacts with understanding, respect and prioritises the same values, you know she's a secure woman who will create peace in your life and is worth pursuing.

7

FOR THE LOVE OF WOMANKIND

"Whatever you give a woman, she will make it greater. If you give her sperm, she'll give you a baby. If you give her a house, she'll give you a home. If you give her groceries, she'll give you a meal. If you give her a smile, she'll give you her heart. She multiplies and enlarges what is given to her. So, if you give her any crap, be ready to receive a tonne of shit!" – Sir William Golding

It'd be bad sportsmanship of me to give a full commentary of the Home team in Chapter 2, without exploring the Away team too, right? So here we have: For the Love of *Woman*kind.

The distinction between male and female is becoming more of a controversial topic as time evolves. We're living in an increasingly polarised society. A rise in open, public debate on topics ranging from transgender rights, to abortion, to identification as non-binary means there is a point to be made by just about everyone – and rightfully so. Unfortunately, human nature is getting the better of us and we're allowing a difference of opinion to pave the way for hatred to take over. Before we know it, we're further from love than we've ever been, with no idea why we're so goddamn tense all the time.

I personally don't think differing opinions is a bad thing, on any topic. It's healthy to put yourself in situations where people disagree with you and challenge you to hear a different perspective. Ultimately, when it comes to men and women, we *shouldn't* be thinking the same way about everything, because we're not the same. We are innately different creatures. And that is beautiful. The differences between the sexes bring balance, fun, variety and love into the world – we should be celebrating that, not letting it divide us!

Real utopia would be love and respect going both ways between men women; for the things one can do that the other can't, for the beliefs held by the other based on their lived experiences, for the way their mind works and their heart loves. Be overcome with admiration for the differences and a desire to learn why they think and behave the way they do, rather than imposing your beliefs onto them. This attitude evolving both ways will see division replaced with harmony.

(31) How do women actually want to be asked out?

There is no right answer here, and of course the perfect way of going about asking a woman on a date will vary depending on the woman, the situation and what you are comfortable with. That is no reason to shy away from it, though. My 'fool proof' advice on this (if there *is* such a thing) is to be led by the idea of 'masculine chivalry'.

What the fuck does that even mean, Marina?!

I hear you. Here comes the explanation:

Despite their differences, most women will be drawn to a guy that takes the lead in this scenario. For the avoidance of doubt, most of us find "we're going to Italiano's at 7pm" *way* more compelling than "umm I don't mind, we can do whatever you want to do." Snooze. We'd far rather the decisive man who is being intentional and clear on wanting to spend time with us, rather than the wet wipe who defaults to *whatever you want to do* and makes *us* do the legwork to arrange plans.

Maybe 'wet wipe' is a bit harsh, given that this version often comes about because you're trying to be considerate of her preferences, or you don't want to decide on the *wrong* thing. But, I'm here to tell you that there's a better way of achieving that well-meant consideration, without coming across as lacklustre. Cue: masculine chivalry.

You start by taking the lead (the *masculine* part of my recipe). Make the plans, telling her when and where. Then give her the space to decide yes or no. You taking decisive action to initiate the plans shows her you *meant it* when you said you wanted to hang out – it's the actions to match the words. That masculine boldness makes a woman feel desired.

However, this *has* to blend with the second ingredient – chivalry. Yes, she wants you to take the lead. But, you need to be a gentleman in doing so, by thinking of her wants, needs and priorities, then building plans around those. That requires asking and listening: What does she value? What interests and excites her? What does she prioritise?

Putting it all together under the neat umbrella of 'masculine chivalry' goes along the lines of:

- "I remember you saying you love authentic street food. I know an amazing Greek stall that opened in a nearby market and I'd love to take you there at 5pm on Saturday. Is that something you'd like and be comfortable doing?"

- "Hey, I'd love to spend time with you on Saturday. I remember you saying you have loads of work to catch up with on Sunday, so I found a cooking workshop we could do at 2pm. That should give us a few hours to enjoy together, and allow you to get home in time for an early night and some rest before Sunday. Does that sound like it'd work for you?"

- "I know that community service is really close to your heart. I'd love to experience that joy with you and see you in your element, so I bought us two aprons and volunteered us to help serve lunch at the local care home on Sunday. Are you up for that?"

Each one comes with a solid plan (the masculine lead) that is intentional about what she enjoys or places value on, and respects her schedule, priorities and boundaries (chivalry). Ta-da! That's the magic combo. *That's* how a woman wants to be asked out. Thank me later.

(32) It's 2023. Isn't chivalry dead?

No, Sir. This mentality is the birthplace of a miserable existence. Regardless of what society, your mates or social media may be telling you, chivalry is not dead. It certainly hasn't stopped being a priority when it comes to what women seek in a man. We need to return to a state whereby having a foundational respect for each other, men and women, is commonplace, encouraged, and our default setting.

Sad as it is, going about your life with a genuine love and respect for women will set you apart in our society. You will stand out as a mature, value-led man who is unafraid to have a presence and set an example. The cherry on top for you? Women are so starved of chivalry these days that, when it does show up, not only are we taken aback, but it's memorable and *so damn sexy.*

I know you're intelligent enough that I don't need to tell you this, but humour me anyway: you came from a woman. Give that the respect it's due. The feminine energy, the way women nurture and what they go through in being our species' *life force* is the most beautiful strength that deserves the *utmost* respect. Humble yourself in genuine appreciation for that. When you do so, you will find that more women want to be around you.

Think for a moment – would you want to be around someone that is disrespectful towards you? Probably not. So you'll be relieved to hear that women are not complicated on this front because we're exactly the same. We don't want to be around a lack or love or respect either. Snap. So, if you really can't muster it then, on behalf of all women: please leave us alone until you've worked on yourself enough that you can.

(33) How do I 'work on myself' and reconnect to that respect for women?

Reflect on the following prompts as a starting point in reconnecting to a mindset of gratitude and respect:

What is beautiful about a woman?

How has a woman contributed to your life?

Whichever female figures come to mind when answering, celebrate those answers. Every woman that has crossed your path is a precious human being in her own right (yes, even your ex)!

She has a family just as special as yours. She has dreams just as big and bold as yours. She has experiences and stories just as rich as yours. She has an internal power just as fierce and formidable as yours. She is not an object to be owned, used, controlled or disposed of, as you see fit. Mate, if you're acting that way, don't be surprised when you get burned by the fire it lights in her.

(34) I do respect women but I don't know what practical things I can do to be a gent and show it?

This definitely isn't something they teach in school. Despite at least 49.5% of the global population (the females!) wanting men to exhibit this kind of behaviour, there are fewer and fewer examples of it out there in the wild to learn from. So I don't begrudge men for asking this question. In fact, I'm relieved when they do. It shows a mature acknowledgement that there's something to be learned and an opportunity to grow.

Plus, it gives me the opportunity to help! Here's some practical bits for you:

- ☑ Offer her your seat in public
- ☑ Offer to carry things for her
- ☑ Offer to pay the bill
- ☑ Hold the door open for her
- ☑ Walk street-side
- ☑ Offer her your coat
- ☑ Pull her chair out for her

These are all generic gestures that you can make to any woman, from family to strangers. No one is going to condemn you for offering to do any of these things. At the core, they're simply good manners and reigniting a respect for women will change your life for the better. After all, you reap what you sew.

However, perhaps you've met her a few times and want to make a slightly more personal chivalrous gesture. Start by asking her to describe the best date she's ever been on. This will give you so much insight into the things that mean a lot to her, and what she finds most impactful or memorable. Taking note, then making a gesture that what means a lot to her will have immeasurable impact. If you're doubting whether your gesture is a bit 'out there', 'weird' or 'too simple', it's not. When your decision-making is directed by what *she* loves and prioritises, you cannot go wrong!

---

(35) What if I do something gentlemanly and it's taken as an insult?

This hesitation is definitely more prevalent since feminist movements such as "Me Too" have become more vocal. By society rightly confronting long-buried feminist issues, many men have become fearful that well-intended chivalry may now offend.

Granted. I will admit that it takes a great deal of courage for a man to be chivalrous these days. You can never really be sure, from one day to the next, what kind of response you'll get from a woman you open the door for, and whether the action will be taken as an insult to her independence.

But, let me level with you for a second. Stop feigning concern as to whether we'd find you *not* letting the door shut in our face offensive. Come on, give us a bit more credit than that. Quite honestly, we have far bigger fish to fry and very few of us are that petty. The truth? Regardless of how independent and powerful a woman is in her own right, most of us agree that if we're going to be around men at all, we'd far rather they be gents than douchebags.

Let me clarify where the lines start to blur.

The issue is not the chivalrous act itself at all. Rather, it's *chivalry with expectation*: doing something gentlemanly for a woman with the expectation that she owes you something in return. That's what really pisses us off.

Worse still is being a Dickhead By Omission (not technically correct legal terminology here, but go with it). This man decides *not* to be chivalrous, *'just in case'*. Just in case things don't work out, he doesn't get the second date, the blowjob, the bragging rights or the promise of a future together.

75

I don't raise this to have a moan. I raise it to help you. As with relationships (and life in general), if your behaviour is dictated by the expectation of a particular outcome, what happens if that outcome doesn't transpire? You're setting yourself up to be disappointed. That disappointment manifests into a simmering resentment that lands you back in a cycle of being a wounded, disconnected man that, frankly, women don't want to be around.

With that said, if you *do* offer her your seat on the train and you're met with a dismissive response or she rejects the offer entirely, you need to understand that that's about *her* and her own wounding. She may react that way for a whole variety of reasons that have *nothing to do with you at all.* Perhaps she's been so hurt in the past that she now lives in a constant survival state of self-defence. Don't let your ego make it about you or use that as an excuse *not* to offer your seat anyway. Do so, then go on with your day feeling good about yourself, because you've been kind to someone without any expectation or knowledge of what internal battles they're fighting.

(36) But not all women *deserve* that chivalrous treatment.

I know there will be a portion of readers thinking that, for whatever reason, a woman may not deserve to benefit from the chivalry you could bless her with. Without the lights and cameras, if you're completely unfiltered and find yourself falling into this boat with your perspective, that is okay. You are not wrong for having your opinion. I want to create an opportunity here for you to reflect. Stop reading and let your thoughts run freely when I ask you:

> *Why* do you feel that some women don't deserve chivalrous treatment?

> What experiences created this mindset in you?

———

Your answers to those questions will forever be your own. That is your truth. However, I take you back to the first woman in your life – your mum. Whatever your journey has been with her, whether tender or turbulent, vulnerable or volatile, I want you to work on forgiving her for whatever has happened along the way. Without knowing either of you personally, I know that every mother does the best she possibly can with the situation she is in. And if nothing else, she gave you life.

Until you start from the beginning, forgive your mother and unpack any residual hurt in that relationship, you will carry on living a disconnected life of hatred for women. Don't carry resentment towards your mother in your heart. Start exploring empathy for her. Ask yourself whether she'd have been a different kind of woman and mother, had she been more supported and nurtured by the men in her life? What if *they'd* stepped up and been a gentleman to her? Acknowledge that possibility, and forgive her.

(37) What does reference to masculine and feminine 'energy' actually *mean*?

In answering this, the best favour I can do for you is to not overcomplicate it. A woman can be letting her 'masculine energy' lead for any number of reasons; maybe she's protecting and providing for her children alone? Maybe she's a sole breadwinner? Maybe she's under intense pressure to deliver for her family, her career or against her own expectations? Whatever her reason for being in that space to begin with, subconscious fear leads many women to become *stuck* in that masculine energy, unable to find softer, more feminine moments.

The key takeaway for you? *You do not need to compete with her for that masculine energy*! Simply do what feels intuitively natural to you and stay solid, consistent and patient. When you do that, she will instinctively soften. Being that masculine 'container' will soothe any subconscious fear, helping her to feel safe enough to let go and drop wholly into her feminine energy. If you want her to grow in her radiance, health, happiness, love, beauty, power and depth, praise these qualities daily. For "praise is literal food for feminine qualities."[25]

How does this feed into the concept of *polarity*?

Polarity is the "opposites attract" idea, whereby you need to embrace your masculine energy if you want to attract feminine energy. There is an element of truth to this. However, we often make the fatal error of ignoring the fact that the polarisation *must* co-exist alongside an ability to *balance* the masculine and feminine energies *within* us all equally.

Why is this so important?

Life will inevitably throw hardship and challenges your way, then demand for you to be more masculine or more feminine, depending on how the situation requires you to step up. You need to be able to tip that scale and pull on the qualities associated with each side, if you're ever going to flourish in the face of adversity.

For example, let's say your wife gets diagnosed with an awful illness. If you cannot balance out your masculine energy with an ability to flow into more feminine traits, what are you going to do? Sit back, all macho, allowing your children to go without a nurturing parental presence in their lives? Be Mr Tough Guy, who lets his wife go through her darkest moments without a compassionate shoulder to cry on? Fuck that.

Avoiding balancing both sides within yourself is a cop-out for the weak. You may miss out on life's most beautiful connections and biggest opportunities because you're unable to lean into your empathy, compassion

---

25   *The Way of the Superior Man*; David Deida (2004).

and intuition. These 'feminine' energies live within us all, regardless of gender. Flowing between them makes you no less of a man. In fact, it actually proves you're able to protect and provide in *whichever* way a situation requires you to. *That* is ultimate strength.

8

THE SUBCONSCIOUS RISE METHOD

We've looked at many different topics through the lens of love, pulling apart different stories we've been told by society and our own subconscious. As I encouraged you to do in the beginning, absorb it all with an open mind and a healthy scepticism, then push yourself to come to your own conclusions, based on a fresh perspective.

Now it's time for The Subconscious Rise Method – how to go from a life of fear to fulfilment. How to know that **love** is at the centre of it all.

(38) Get out of your head and into your heart.

We live in a world where the "head" stuff tends to consume us. Too often, we're completely and unquestioningly led by how society tells us things should be. And that tends to birth a whole lot of judgement, both of ourselves and everyone else. We judge things when they're not *done* the way they 'should be'. We judge people for not *being* the way they 'should be'. That judgement pisses me off. Let it piss you off too.

What is the need for it? Does it get us ahead? Does it make us feel good inside? Does it help us create beauty and connection in our lives? Does judgement make us rate ourselves higher when we look in the mirror?

It's bollocks. Living in our own heads means we're missing out on the present, the gifts in life and opportunities to go *deeper*. All because we're allowing our lives to be led by false information. Wake up, sleeper. That misleading societal 'standard' has you perpetually chasing happiness, thinking it's everywhere *but* the present. Chasing an illusion. Not exactly cruising for success…

Life shouldn't be about idolising others or blindly following what they're doing with their appearance, career, clothes, love life or anything else. It's about being present and finding fulfilment, right where you are. Being stuck in your own head will distract you from that. Only centring yourself and re-connecting to your heart will keep you on the path to fulfilment.

To plug in to your heart, set yourself an intentional routine; a daily promise to yourself to be the hero of your story, not to let anyone but *you* play the main character in your life. This routine promise can take any form and there is no right or wrong way of setting the intention. You can even think of it as a wedding vow to yourself, pledged with the same gravity and soulful intention. If you're unsure where to start or what to do, simply hold your hands together and speak aloud.

You can either repeat this prayerful adaptation exactly, or change it to match your needs:

I am not a body.

I am free.

For I am perfect and I was created by God.

May I use all of my gifts to serve humanity.

I am peace.

> ***Peace is who I am.***
>
> Return to silence. Imagine your body turning into light and shining love and healing on any parts of you that need attention and care.
>
> Then imagine that light shining outwards to your friends, family and those who are suffering, engulfing them in a bright and blinding love.
>
> Ask God to help guide you through the day ahead.[26]

(39) Love the Fuck out of Everything.

Love yourself. Love the turbulent experiences you've had and the battles you've overcome. They made you you. It's much easier to blame everyone else for the things you've been through, to play into the victimhood and stories surrounding these situations. But you now have a fresh outlook that recognises those 'stories' are all bullshit. Grab your life in both hands and decide what story you're going to tell yourself, from now on. Rewrite the script the way *you* want it to be. And for fuck's sake, you might as well write a good one!

Love the pain you've endured and overcome. Pain is a part of life, even if you see it coming. That won't ever change, so wasting time trying to predict or avoid pain by running from it is pointless. You'll need more than a few Red Bulls to run from that one… Instead, choose to *love* that pain for the strength it led you to find within, for the lessons it taught you and for the joy you now appreciate more.

Instead of wallowing, choose to *love* the people that hurt you along the way, and the things you've done to hurt yourself. I promise, you will

---

26   Adapted from: *A Course in Miracles*; Helen Schuman (1976).

never be on your death bed regretting giving 100% to a situation or being kind to someone. Doing so will, at the very least, allow you to take a legendary leap forwards, feeling proud of the man in the mirror and knowing that you will begin attracting more positive, loving energy because that is the way you're choosing to *be*.

(40) Slow down. Stillness is food for the senses.

I want to hammer home how important it is to make space in your life. Build in space to slow down. And build physical spaces that *awaken* all five senses. I'm the first to admit that this can seem much easier said than done, but an easy place to start is by getting out in nature. Smell the grass. Hear the birds. Feel the ground beneath your feet. Taste the fresh air. See the surrounding beauty. I mean, *really* take it all in – all that... *peace*.

Why am I saying that creating sensory stillness is so vital? Yes, it gives you time to reflect amongst the bustle of daily to-do lists. But more importantly, it has physiological benefit. It allows your nervous system to recognise 'safety' and release out of 'fight or flight' mode.

When you think about it, we have extremely few spaces that calm all our senses in modern life. The vast majority of us are working, socialising, exercising and even meeting new people in physical settings that put our senses on high-alert. It's brightly-lit and noisy offices, bars, clubs and busy gyms.

Whilst there is nothing wrong with these places, they are not healing environments in themselves. More often than not, these spaces foster total disconnect. However, if we *do* manage to connect to ourselves or the people we meet there, those connections will most likely be built on a chaotic foundation. It's not the calm, peaceful kick-off that will fulfil us long-term. In other words, we're not setting ourselves up for success if we neglect to put ourselves in spaces of sensory harmony.

'Sensory harmony' seems illusive. How do I achieve that?

A good place to start is to focus on reconnecting with your body, rather than trying to escape it. The spiritual world is crowded with people advocating for mushrooms, DMT and anything else that will get you *out* of your body. Fuck that. There's far more to be said for grounding *into* it.

This isn't just some 'woowoo' idea I came up with on the loo. Giving birth to my second child allowed me to experience first-hand the sheer power and brute strength that comes from getting out of your head and grounding into your heart and body. I was able to time the birth down to the minute, successfully delivering my child at home, without any pain medication at all. How? It was two-fold.

I created a *physical* space at home that put all five of my senses at ease. Then I created a *mental* space of peace and calmness through hypnosis and visualisation. Repeatedly listening to hypnosis tracks and rehearsing visualisation exercises before going to sleep every night was monumental. I got physical proof of these techniques when I went from being someone who'd take a paracetamol for the slightest headache, to someone that gave birth without even so much as gas and air. But these techniques proved to be *mentally* transformative too. In devoting myself to practicing daily, I had reprogrammed my subconscious mind so powerfully that I re-framed my mother's negative narrative of childbirth into it being the best, most rawly beautiful experience for both my children and I.

By no means am I saying these techniques took the pain away, by *any* stretch. I'm not here to lie to you by painting life as being all love, peace and rainbows. Things are painful, angry and really fucking shit sometimes. We didn't sign up to be a robot that doesn't feel pain. We're human.

So yes, channel the powerful, positive energy that comes from embracing love. But 'Love *the Fuck* out of Everything' because you've got to remember to pack a punch in there sometimes too. *Let* things hurt. Let shit affect you. Just do so in a safe place around people that have your best interests at heart. You *need* to let it in and surrender to it, in order to give it the love and gratitude it deserves, before you're able to move through it and let it go. Without the surrender, you'll only attract *more* pain.

This has real substance and produces real, life-changing results. Miss out at your own risk.

A SIMPLE SUMMARY

You don't need to be giving birth or going through some kind of transformative experience to pick up the remote and change the channel from your head to your heart. Come as you are, wherever you're at in your life, and experiment with different techniques until you find the ones that leave you feeling a little bit lighter than when you started.

To help you get to a point where you *can* Love the Fuck out of Everything, here's a helpful summary of things you can try, based on what we've covered in the book, with page references next to each. A lightbulb moment will be sparked be a completely different approach or technique, from one reader to the next. So flick around to recap and find what works for you.

9

GODSPEED

God-Speed – not on your timeline

Learning to wholly love yourself, your circumstances and others will rebuild you. Quite literally – the serotonin amplifies growth hormones that make you look younger and more beautiful. So, have a plan. Fuck the fear and take action! For if you don't *look* for the good in life, it is guaranteed you won't find it.[27]

But remember: Rome wasn't built in a day. Have patience and give yourself grace along the way. To be human is to be in a state of continuous evolution and learning. Like a fine wine, you are not trying to arrive at a specific *destination* or outcome – there is no 'drink by' date. Instead, strive for a journey through life that only gets fuller and richer the longer you're lucky enough to live it.

Godspeed – for the start of a journey

"Th[e] passage, from who we used to be to who we are capable of becoming, is the greatest hope for healing of the human race."[28]

You're done reading and it's time to start doing. You're taken the first step in reading with an open mind, now you have a unique, beautiful and no-doubt challenging journey ahead of you in which you will further build out your own opinions and actually *take action*.

---

27   A wonderful life lesson from my Dad, Athos Lazaris.
28   *Conversations with God;* Neale Donald Walsch (2006)

Your inner Legend is now the pilot. He is going to fly your plane with grace, honour and respect. It will be a smooth journey, because turbulent energy is met by a strong sense of self, an appreciation for differences, and love for the growth, learning and beauty that comes from pain and challenges. He unashamedly recognises when he goes wrong or needs guidance, and will seek information from the trusted few with front row seats at air traffic control, who will selflessly get him back on his intended path.

And when he needs to let go altogether, he doesn't believe he's failed, because he has a 100% success rate in surviving everything he's been through so far. Instead, he knows he's done a great job with the skills, knowledge and tools he's had at each point, and confidently switches on auto-pilot. The auto-pilot is now reprogrammed with his core values and safely takes the lead until he's through the clouds, cruising at altitude. Peace. Stillness. Untainted beauty. Unbridled love and gratitude for where he is and how he's gotten there.

This is what he came for. *This* was the goal. He is fulfilled.

DEDICATIONS

DEDICATED TO ALL THE PHENOMENAL MEN THAT HAVE IMPACTED MY LIFE AND INSPIRED ME, EACH OF YOU UNIQUELY ENTREPRE-NEURIAL, ECCENTRIC, CHIVALROUS, LOVING AND MASCULINE.

ATHOS LAZARIS, Dad, the most extroverted, eccentric and inspiring man I've ever known. Thank you for giving me pure, unconditional love. You are an inspiring example of unrelenting self-belief and determination to sail your life's ship *your* way. Despite your journey being littered with obstacles that would defeat most, you not only became an entrepreneurial success story, but turned life's most painful experiences into an abundance of positivity. I will forever admire you for that. My biggest cheerleader and first teacher of spiritual experiences, thank you for empowering me to make my own way in the world with my head held high. You taught me that life is about the person you're being in your soul, not how much you earn, how you look or anything external. That lesson was one of the biggest blessings in my life. I couldn't have prayed for a better, kinder or more loving father. You've impacted my life in more ways that words can express. I love you.

MR ROLLS, you were the first person to champion my acting. Your insistence for me to play Queen Victoria, despite my fear, was the first time someone believed I could so something when I didn't believe it myself. Thank you for giving me the push I needed, for that was the beginning of a passion that's lasted me a lifetime. *"Hey Albie, baby!"*

CHRISTODOULOS KOFTEROS (DADDA), what a man you are. Thank you for loving me as another godchild and accepting me fully for who I am, with open arms and zero expectation. On countless occasions, you've captivated me completely – with your amazing storytelling, your phenomenal business mind and unconditional generosity. Thank you for wrapping me in warmth, chivalry and laughter, and demonstrating an amazing marriage with Tina. With your infectious energy and zest for life, you are every essence of what a man should be.

STEVEN TOUMBAS, you made a first impression on me that long out-lasted your short life. Even at such a young age, you were the first boy I met who protected and stuck up for me so instinctively. An old soul in a young body, you were the brightest spark in any room and had the most admirable emotional intelligence and selfless respect for women. Thank you for being such a genuine friend and wanting the best for me. I will always cherish our shared laughter, your boundless charisma and hunger to such an abundant life.

ANDREAS ANDROU, thank you for telling me I was loved every single day, for teaching me what securely attached love felt like. Thank you for giving me the wings to leave you and, in doing so, teaching me to never betray who I am for the love of someone else. I will forever respect you for the proactive and present father you are to our daughters. Thank you.

STEVE HARDISON, you are the embodiment of authenticity, a leader that is unafraid to do things his own way and forge his own path. And you do so with the utmost grace and kindness towards everyone you encounter.

While I've never a better listener than you, it was your chivalry that impacted me most. The way you live a full, modern life while upholding such beautiful values when it comes to respect for women just blows me away. Thank you for being one of the only people to *really* listen to me, deeply, and for teaching me to never idolise anyone because we're all human.

VICTOR BOC, we have the purest friendship that blossomed out of nowhere. We've shared many fun experiences together, from Zoom dance parties to podcast creation. You demonstrate so wonderfully that you get what you give in life. Thank you for allowing me to experience such a perfectly reciprocal relationship. You are an angel that fills my cup with light and fun. Thank you for being such an avid supporter of mine.

MATT KAHN, I cannot thank you enough for helping me see the value in being myself. Your kindness and commitment to staying in love, despite life's turbulence, has such a profound impact on me. Thank you for being such a fun, vibrational mirror to my soul, and keeping it real with me every step of the way! I will forever treasure your honesty and humour.

LINDSAY BRADY, you are a remarkably wise soul with that exudes so much light. You've taught me so much more than hypnosis – thank you for being my philosophical teammate and our time spent intellectualising the spiritual and scientific crossroads within human consciousness.

ISIAH HANKEL, your entrepreneurial message to stand up for yourself and stop apologising for who you are in this world has been a source of inspiration to me for a long time. Since meeting many years ago, you have been instrumental in helping the entrepreneur in me blossom. For that I cannot thank you enough. I will be forever grateful for the strong conviction you've had in me and my message.

LEONID FROLOV; on one hand, my Certification coach. On the other hand, the most gentle, kind soul. You taught me that I can be soft and gentle in an oftentimes hard world. Thank you for being consistent in your unconditional love and holding space for me, no matter how I showed up. And thank you for your guidance in the completion of this book. You pour such a bright light into both my life and the world.

NEALE DONALD WALSCH, my favourite author of all time, thank you for authentically sharing your conversations with God with the world. You enabled me to reconnect with God's true message that we are all One. I will always hold your words close to my heart; *"Marina, if not now then when? If not you, then who?"* Everyone has a gift in this world, thank you for reminding me to use mine.

KIM HARDY PHOTOGRAPHY; Kim, you are the best photographer I've worked with to date. Thank you for shooting me in a way that so wonderfully blended acting (specifically the Meisner technique) with fostering genuine trust. Your kind, eccentric nature made me feel more like 'me' than I have in any other shoot, whilst your passion for your art really brought out my soul. I've never been so sparked by a photoshoot. Thank you for reminding me why I love acting so much and delivering such beautiful, authentic photography.

THANK YOU NOTE

Karen Mason: EMDR Consultant

Karen, thank you for your fierce, lioness love. You took me under your wing, felt my anger alongside me, and helped me release through EMDR. You are a strong, powerful woman who is amazing to work with and has a beautiful heart to match.

Rachel Ward: NAET

Rachel, thank you for being judgement-free and working with me around my the beliefs behind my allergies. You are one of the kindest, most beautiful and gentle souls I've ever met.

Amanda Douglas: Kinesiology

Amanda, thank you for gracing my life with your empathetic, nurturing, stable and consistent female presence. Working with you has been such an honour. You taught me that a shift in emotion can come as a sigh and helped me release illness from my body.

Annie Jenkins: Kinesiology

Annie, thank you for the beautiful experience of sharing space with you as I worked through some of the earlier traumas I held in my body. You are an eccentric kinesiologist with the sweetest and loveliest nature, and I'm so grateful for your guidance.

Herbal Inn Acupuncture, Dr Gao

From just feeling the pulses in my hands to understanding what was going on with my body and helping me release it, Herbal Inn is without a doubt the best acupuncturist I've ever used. Absolutely phenomenal and I can't thank you enough.

Dao Tran-Boyd: Sound Healing

Dao, thank you for the immersive experience you created by putting sound healing bowls on my body. You allowed me to journey into different lifetimes. The stillness and simplicity of the space you held for me was incredible and left such a profound impact on me.

Steven Bannister: Breathwork facilitation

Steven, you helped me to breathe deeply into different parts of my body in order to release stuck emotion and energy. Thank you for leaving a career in the City to create a beautiful space for the facilitation of breathwork. You are such a kind, gentle and nurturing man and I am so grateful to have experienced working with you.

Alejandro Martin: Designer

Alejandro Martin, thank you for your kindness and professionalism with all of the book edits. You went above and beyond to ensure all of the edits were done in a professional and timely manner.

ABOUT MARINA

You're here because you have all the ingredients society said you needed to be happy. Except the happiness. I get it.

You see, I wasn't always a Relationship coach. My life has had its' fair share of turbulence and adversity. I've been confused too – lost in society's conflicting web of 'how to win at life' and 'how to be loved'. I'd fucked myself over. I sought love everywhere but within. I didn't understand that love is something you *are*, not something you *get*. At one point in my life, being born on Valentine's Day was…ironic…at best.

So, how did I get here? I worked a corporate career spanning senior sales, training and development for over 20 years, pursuing professional acting throughout. During that journey, I spent every day recognising the needs of the audience in front of me, connecting to what makes them tick. I developed a knack for finding the treasure in every tale. I fell in love with the idea that every person can have a spotlight in this world. And that I could make that happen for them.

Cue, career change.

I studied psychodynamic counselling and achieved accreditation in mindfulness and hypnosis methodologies.

In 2014, I combined all of this and founded The Subconscious Rise Method: the intersection of psychology, neuro-linguistic programming, acting and hypnosis.

As a Certified Co-active Coach, I have led entrepreneurs, CEOs and many more back to authentic, fulfilled lives by putting love centre-stage. Trust me, we all have our shit. You are not alone. I'm a pro at turning that 'shit' into the force that drives a life you're proud of. A life powered by inner-strength and bursting with momentum. The life you deserve.

I've never enjoyed work so much because I get to pull back the curtains of confusion and conflict within my clients. They learn how to access a new level of depth that amplifies empathy, emotional intelligence and self-trust. They now follow the script written by their core values. Their body is the only costume they wear. They're fully connected to who they are, and they're able to *breathe* again. Peace. True freedom. Love. THAT's my mission.

My mission is to unmask society's lies and eliminate shame, so you can live a fully-integrated, heart-centred life. Arriving at my 40th birthday this Valentine's Day, I want to share my personal lessons about the world of love, sex and relationships. My longing is for you to realise that you are already the legend you've always wanted to be. I hope that sharing my thoughts and guidance in a simple, candid way answers your biggest questions and helps you reach your own, balanced conclusions on the way to living a full, connected life. And who knows? Maybe you even laugh along the way…

Printed in Dunstable, United Kingdom

66358046R00060